Fighting For Russ:
Life After Anoxic Brain Injury

By

Diane Cesarz Lockwood

To God, whose divine intervention reaffirmed the gift of life

To my daughter, Stephanie, whose constant support and love sustained me in my darkest hours

To my friends and neighbors- Arlene, Kip, Amanda, Ed and Roxanne, Katie, Bill P, Judy, Jill, Jodi and Bill. Your kindness and help was appreciated, more than you know.

Preface

April 11-This date would forever change my life. Before then, I was busy working 60 hours a week, leaving little time for anything else. However, I did find time on the weekends to enjoy my husband. Even doing the mundane things like going to the home improvement store to look for the latest tool which he just had to have or helping him build our deck was the chance to reconnect with him. We led a simple, happy life. After my husband's cardiac arrest and subsequent anoxic brain injury, our everyday life changed. Suddenly it was up to me alone to make decisions about his care while at the same time managing our household finances and dealing with a lawn tractor that wouldn't start or rotors which needed to be replaced in our car. There were endless daily trips to the hospital and later the nursing home. I'd spend most of the day there, leaving by early evening to attend to our pets and get some sleep myself. My daily routine had a new meaning.

The title of this book, *Fighting For Russ,* implies that the author is a fighter. My persona is quite the opposite of a fighter. Most people perceive me as laid-back and quiet (something they feel compelled to point out). I suppose professionals would label me an introvert

.

But I would call up another facet of my being: an inner tenacity to endure a living hell and somehow maintain my sanity. I called upon God to give me strength and strength he did give me to get through every difficult day. Even though I do not make friends easily, I am intensely loyal to those friends I do have. My husband is my best friend. I became his voice and learned to be his advocate: something an intensive care nurse advised me to do when he was released from the hospital.

We never know how high we are
Till we are asked to rise
And then if we are true to plan
Our statures reach the sky-

Emily Dickinson

My husband is not a high- ranking public official or medical professional with an array of resources. In fact, he survived against overwhelming odds and with limited resources. All therapy was short-lived in the nursing home and continued for only a few months upon his release to our home. I then took over the role of therapist, learned from watching and repeating what the actual physical therapist had done.

This book is about a common man who survived what few do, a cardiac arrest. He was a blue-collar worker most of his life. When he retired, instead of sitting around at home he enjoyed doing yard work for others. His humor and outgoing personality made him popular around the neighborhood. He liked helping others and would assist the older residents with chores.

According to the Heart Rhythm Foundation, sudden cardiac arrest accounts for about 325,000 deaths each year. Less than 10% of people survive a cardiac arrest. My husband is one of the few who survived. This is his story.

April 11

   This day starts out like most of my busy days. It begins with the sudden blare of the alarm clock rousing me out of a sound sleep. My blurry morning eyes make out the time, 5:45 am. I turn off the alarm and look at Russ who has squirmed at the violent noise. He has now been retired for 18 months and enjoys the luxury of more sleep. But now the dog's pacing and the cat meowing for her breakfast remind me of my morning responsibilities. After a shower, getting dressed and a quick breakfast of a cereal bar, I head out the door. It's going to be an adjustment going back to work since being off the previous week for Spring break. I leave work at 3:30 and proceed to my 2nd job at the library from 4-8pm. These 12-hour days last 4 days a week so by Friday evening I can be found falling asleep in the recliner under my throw blanket. Russ teases me when I reach for the throw and comments that I will soon be asleep.

   Upon finishing our late dinner, I ask Russ how things went during the day. He had a heart attack on April 5 and spent 3 days in the hospital. I've had to caution him not to overdo it. He has been feeling good and wants to stay active. Next week he has an appointment at the cardiac rehabilitation center where they will start him on an exercise program. Today, he applied fertilizer to a neighbor's yard. Russ does lawn maintenance for our many older neighbors and keeps track of the billing on Microsoft Excel. Although he never had any formal instruction in computers, he taught himself how to use many programs. His sharp mind and strong hands helped him run this business. Our deck and the carport were projects that he successfully completed. I again remind him not to do too much. At 9:45pm, I go into the bedroom and settle down in bed after my long day. I leave Russ in the living room where he watches pro wrestling, something I have no interest in. A few minutes later, just as I am on the verge of sleep, Russ comes in the bedroom to ask me if I would like chicken or spaghetti for dinner tomorrow He usually cooks dinner for us. I choose the chicken. He moves close to my head and kisses me good night. As he turns to leave the bedside, he suddenly falls.

Without any warning, Russ has collapsed on the floor. I have the "deer in the headlights" reaction at first, the kind that elicits a type of frozen fear. . Then some force throws me back into reality and I shake him, calling his name. He is lying face down in the narrow space between the bed and dresser but I manage to feel for a carotid pulse, nothing! I think *oh God, this can't be happening.* I fumble to find a pulse elsewhere, on the wrist. Still nothing. I attempt to turn him over to do CPR but because of the narrow space and his ample weight, my struggle is in vain. I can't waste time doing this. He's not breathing! I run to the phone and call 911. Somehow I tell them the story and the dispatcher keeps me on the line, distracting me with questions like, is he still breathing? How long ago did it happen? Even so, my heart is racing and I'm shaking with fear. I hear the distant wail of a siren and know they are on their way. It seems like an eternity. *Hurry, hurry I pray.* Suddenly, several emergency vehicles converge out front at the end of

6

our entry sidewalk. 3 emergency personnel run to the front door where I direct them to the bedroom. They are carrying equipment including an AED, which they immediately use on Russ. I stay in the kitchen trembling all the while. Another first responder arrives and asks how I am doing. I reply, "I'm scared" between my shaking and tears. He tells me that Russ is in good hands. I do realize that and am grateful for their help. Another 4 responders arrive and go into the bedroom. After a few minutes, a first responder tells me that Russ now has a heart rhythm and pulse. He asks which hospital I prefer and I tell them the downtown hospital. They say that I can ride along in the ambulance but I decline and say I will drive myself. Again they ask how I am doing. "I'm managing" is my reply. I steady myself enough to safely drive to the hospital, all the time wondering if he'll be all right and blaming myself for not being able to do more for him.

    At the emergency room, I tell the desk staff that my husband arrived there by ambulance. I am directed to sit in the waiting room. After a few minutes, a nurse escorts me to an exam room where Russ is connected to a barrage of wires, machines and IV's. I immediately begin to cry at the sight. A chaplain comes in and asks if there is anyone who can sit with me. Really, the only person that comes to mind is Stephanie, my daughter. I don't have any family members here in town but Stephanie is 9 months pregnant and lives in Virginia. The chaplain leads me to a nearby quiet room. It has several chairs and has the appearance of a small waiting room. Together we hold hands and pray for Russ. She leaves, saying she is going to check on Russ. I am still shaking. When she returns, she tells me that Russ is being taken to 4

East, the cardiac intensive care unit. I can go to the waiting room there where a doctor will talk to me. She asks if I want her to come with me. I tell her no since I need to collect my thoughts. She hands me her business card and says to call if I need someone to talk to.

April 12

I make my way to a small, dimly lite waiting room just outside of 4 East. It consists of a vinyl loveseat, a matching chair and a computer. I feel so alone with only the racing thoughts in my head. *Will Russ make it? What kind of permanent damage will he suffer? Could I have done more?* I now think about Russ's children. I will have to call them but it's 12:16 am so I decide to wait until later in the morning. I am still teary-eyed and the emotional stress makes my body feel even more fatigued. At 1:30, I am startled by quick footsteps coming into the room. The doctor tells me that Russ is in a coma and is on a ventilator. He has consent forms for me to sign, one to insert a central line and the other for therapeutic hypothermia. He explains that the therapeutic hypothermia consists of cooling the body for 24 hrs and then gradually warming it back up. Patients who are given this treatment have better outcomes. It is used for cardiac arrest and drowning incidents. The doctor says Russ is stable and encourages me to go home to get some rest. Although I am reluctant to leave, I remember that I still need to call work to report my absence. The phone number is at home so I leave. At 2:10am, even the downtown streets of my small city are devoid of any sign of human life, adding to my isolation.

I pull in the driveway at 2:30 and after setting my alarm for 5:45, I lay in bed crying for the next half hour. *God, give me strength.* What follows is a few hours of tossing and turning, not sleeping or resting. At 5:45, I call the principal at school and tearfully tell her that my husband has had a cardiac arrest. She tells me to take as much time as I need. I thank her and head back to the hospital.

April 13

When I get back to the hospital, I find Russ still unresponsive but after looking at the steady rhythm of the heart monitor, I find comfort that at least his heart is beating. At 9:00 am the medical team is making their visits to the cardiac patients. They are now in the room next door. After a few minutes they stop outside Russ's room and close the sliding entry door, to probably discuss his case, away from inquisitive ears. The team appears to consist of doctors, interns, therapists and nurses. When the doctor enters the room, he explains how the therapeutic hypothermia works. The cooling machine is at the foot of the bed with inflatable chambers filled with water on Russ's legs. Tomorrow they will remove these and gradually warm his body temperature back up. Hopefully, this will minimize any brain damage. They are giving Russ medication for his heart since as the doctor puts it *the heart doesn't like being that cold.* It's still too early to predict any outcome. At 11:00am, I call Russ's oldest daughter in Illinois to inform her of the situation. I stress the seriousness of his condition although I have very few answers as of now. She says she will tell the other family members and head here to see him. I also call my daughter, Stephanie, to assess her of the situation. She is now on maternity leave and is at home. She wishes she could be here but I tell her to take it easy and keep Russ in her prayers.

The nurses come in to turn Russ as they've done every 2 hrs. After the second nurse leaves, the first one asks if she can get me anything. I decline but ask where the nearest bathroom is. I take a short break and walk to the cafeteria where I eat a small salad. I do feel so very alone. My lack of sleep and the emotional stress is making me exhausted but I need to stay here longer. Perhaps this cup of coffee will buy me more time.

I return to the room where a nurse is checking Russ's vital signs. After she leaves, I look at Russ. My once strong husband lies here so vulnerable and dependent on monitors, a ventilator, IVs for his very existence. I turn his crisis over to God and know that he will be in good hands. Finally at 7:00 pm, after being awake for more than 24 hrs, my fatigue overwhelms me and I realize that I need sleep. I manage to drive home, by keeping the window open and allowing the cool April breeze to keep me somewhat alert. At home, the answering machine emits a beeping sound, indicating that I have messages. There are 8 messages, which I listen to. However, I am too exhausted to call anyone back. That will be my task for tomorrow. Today, the need for sleep overwhelms me and I quickly fall asleep.

April 14

When I arrive at the hospital, I learn that Russ has had a seizure during the night. The doctor explains that this is quite common, adding that he has given Russ Phenobarbital, an anti- seizure medication. My mother, an epileptic, took this medication for many years. There is an EEG machine attached to Russ, which continuously monitors the brain for seizure activity. He is not reacting to any stimulus and this worries me. It's only been a short time since his cardiac arrest though and I must remain hopeful. I take a break to call neighbors and friends who are concerned about Russ. Our next-door neighbors said that they saw the ambulance in front of our house and were wondering what was going on. I explained the situation and they say they will start a prayer chain for Russ. Other neighbors also will keep him in their prayers. Russ's friend Bill said that he would let the dog out for me.

At mid-morning, Russ's sister from a nearby town comes in to see him and keep me company. Later in the afternoon, his daughter from out of town arrives. Her siblings will also soon arrive. The medical professionals are now warming Russ's body, as part of the therapeutic hypothermia. He is still attached to a significant amount of various clear plastic IV bags and with them the only sound is the high-pitched beep coming from a monitor. I again pray for any improvement. He is now taken away to have a CAT scan. All of Russ's children are now here. I tell them what little I know. They stay for a few hours, saying they will return later. Our next-door neighbors come to visit along with our good friend, Bill. Russ remains comatose with no response and tightly closed eyes.

April 15
    I am now in a new routine of arriving at the hospital at 8am and staying until 8pm. The doctors and the team do rounds at around 9am so I make sure I'm here to talk to them. Russ's sister comes in at 10am to again see him and keep me company. I am very grateful for her companionship. The nurse tells us that Russ had an uneventful night. She adds that they will remove the EEG monitor since there were no further seizures. He is doing some whole body twitching and I ask her about that. She says that it is quite common for someone in his condition. Russ's son was here in the middle of the night, according to the nurse. He stayed for a while and went to his aunt's house to get some sleep.

April 16
    There is another day of watching and waiting for some response, any response. The good news is that Russ has not had any more seizures. The therapeutic hypothermia is complete and only time will tell its effectiveness. He does have compression boots on his legs to prevent blood clots. Several family members visit including Russ's son who is refreshed after getting some sleep. He and Russ's stepson go outside for a cigarette break. As she has done since the hospitalization, Stephanie calls to see how Russ and I are doing. She realizes how difficult this is on me so she calls every day. It is her calls and concern that are getting me through this. I'm very lucky in that she is the kind of daughter most people

would love to have. After the others leave, I again pray and turn Russ's recovery over to God.

April 17

I am at the hospital early so I can see how Russ is doing before I leave to pick up Russ's sister, Kip, who lives in California. She called earlier in the week and offered to stay with me for a month. It will be good to have some company. She's been special to me ever since Russ and I got married 10 years ago in her backyard. She worked hard then, making the decorations and ensuring that we had a wedding to remember. Before I leave, I notice that Russ's eyes are open a little but the whites are bloodshot. The doctor goes through the daily task of commanding Russ to wiggle his toes, squeeze the doctor's hand and open his eyes. There is no response from Russ. *Please, Russ, please you can do it.* I am disappointed. However, I can sense that he is struggling to survive and that's all I can hope for now. I pick Kip up at the airport early in the afternoon and brief her on Russ's condition. Later in the afternoon, Russ's other sister visits along with Bill and Jenny. Our next-door neighbors visit to check on Russ's condition. They bring a casserole for Kip and I to enjoy later. I am getting word of neighborhood rumors that say Russ is brain dead. This really angers me. If people want to know how he is doing, why don't they just contact me instead of starting crazy rumors. I decide that I will post a weekly progress report in the community clubhouse so everyone will know the facts.

April 18

For the past week, I have kept my cell phone on the nightstand beside me in case the hospital calls. At 4:00 am, the ring suddenly awakens me. I answer it with trepidation, hoping it isn't the hospital with bad news. The voice on the other end is Neil, my son-in-law with the news that he and Stephanie are the new parents of a baby girl, Karina, who was born at 3:00 am. I ask how Stephanie is doing and Neil tells me that she is exhausted but doing well. He says that Karina is 7lbs, 7oz with a lot of dark hair. I then realize that today, April 18th, is Russ's birthday too. What a wonderful affirmation of life that he and Karina now share the same birthday. I so desperately need some good news and this invigorates me.

When Kip and I arrive at the hospital, I tell Russ the good news. Somehow I think he'll understand. I pin the birthday card I got him on his bulletin board. The card takes on a special meaning in that he has survived long enough to have another birthday. When the doctor examines Russ, he is concerned about the rigidity in Russ's arms and how they turn in. He again commands Russ to open his eyes, squeeze his hand, and wiggle his toes. There is no response. He then tells Kip and I that Russ has a 5-10% chance of recovery. I say nothing but in my heart I know that he is wrong. I know Russ and am convinced that he will survive. Bill arrives later with a birthday card, a balloon and some artificial flowers since real flowers aren't allowed in the cardiac intensive unit. These also go on the bulletin board. A neighbor, Don, calls to see how things are going.

Several neighbors stop in later to visit. Russ's grandson and his girlfriend stop in and bring a birthday balloon. Other family members arrive and soon the room is crowded with Russ's family. It gets noisy with all the people talking. The chatter starts to annoy and overwhelm me although I am grateful that they have come to visit. *Can Russ hear all this? Does he know what's going on?* Russ's sister talks about how she and her husband will soon open their pool and start grilling. I am a little envious into this glimpse of a normal life. For the past week, my life has been turned upside down and I can hardly remember what normal activities feel like. The visitors begin to trickle out. I welcome the silence.

April 19

Before I leave for the hospital, Stephanie calls to say that she is a little tired but feels good. She put a picture of Karina on Facebook . I print the picture out to put on Russ's bulletin board. I also put another picture of her on the refrigerator. Just looking at her picture brightens my day. She is a joy to me. I am proud to have her in my life today and for many more years to come.

Kip and I have breakfast in the hospital cafeteria as we've had for the past few days and head up to 4E in time for the doctor's rounds. As before, the doctor loudly commands Russ to open his eyes, squeeze his hand and wiggle his toes. He astounds us by doing all three tasks. Kip and I are elated, so much so, that tears of joy well up in our eyes. It seems like a great weight has been lifted off our shoulders. The doctor is more reserved to this response. No matter what, I am convinced that Russ will recover, although I know he has a long road ahead of him. We call family members to tell them the good news.

We leave the hospital at 5:30 pm to have dinner with one of my co-workers who was kind enough to invite us to her home, which is only a block from the hospital. Before the meal, we join hands and pray for Russ's recovery. The dinner of grilled pork, mashed potatoes and green beans is a welcome change from the hospital food we've had. We savor each bite as if it were our last meal. Finally, my supervisor from work calls to see how everything is and tells me that the office will send paperwork for a FMLA. I am grateful that she is so understanding. Kip and I return to the cardiac intensive care unit to find Russ in his deep sleep. It's been another long day for us so we head home to get some rest ourselves.

April 20

At 2:00 am, I am awakened by the sound of my cell phone ringing. It's the hospital saying that Russ's heart had stopped again. They did a full code on him and got the heart beating again. He is stable. I wake up Kip and we head for the hospital. Russ is resting comfortably, unaware of the drama. Kip settles in the reclining chair while I search out the other reclining chair in the nearby lounge area. Kip and I want to stay close to Russ for the night. It is silent in the lounge area except for the occasional page or staff member walking past me. Usually this area is full of anxious family members but tonight I am alone and the empty vastness does little to comfort me. Again, I silently pray for Russ's life. Before long my fatigue overwhelms me into a light sleep. At 8am I return to the room and find Kip awake. We decide to take a break and get something to eat downstairs. When the medical team arrives, the doctor asks me if I want a Do Not Resuscitate in Russ's chart. Without hesitating, I say no, I want a full code. Although the heart stoppage was disappointing, I know that he will recover. After rounds, Russ's sister visits for an hour while Kip and I maintain our vigil. Kip does word searches and I write in my journal. I've written in the journal daily since Russ was admitted. I really think it helps maintain my sanity, to write my thoughts down. The nurses come in frequently to check Russ's vital signs and to turn him, every 2 hours. They also clean his mouth with a type of spongy toothbrush. I can tell that he dislikes this because he moves his head from side to side in an attempt to get away from it. His eyes are open but still bloodshot. Kip and I take several breaks to get lunch and visit the gift shop. After a long, difficult day we leave for home at 8pm.

April 21

Today Russ has a PEG tube, otherwise known as a stomach tube inserted. Although it is an invasive procedure, it is necessary so he can get nourishment and recover as well as possible. He is unaware of the drama. This will allow the medical staff to give him liquid feedings through the tube. Kip and I leave while the doctor inserts the tube. Russ has tolerated the procedure well. Most of the IVs have been removed. He is also coughing which the nurse says is important to remove any secretions. To me it's another sign of Russ coming back to life. Stephanie continues to call me daily. Her support makes this nightmare bearable.

April 22

There is an important milestone for Russ today. He is removed from the ventilator and has a tracheotomy done. A tube is attached to the tracheotomy, the opening in his throat, and this long clear tube leads to a machine that supplies him with supplemental oxygen. Russ's daughter and son-in-law visit. I didn't know they were coming back from out of town. But I am grateful that they are here. Kip and I leave at 8:00pm after another long but productive day.

April 23

Today my sister Chris and her husband Charlie arrive from Chicago to visit Russ and see how I am doing. It means so much to have them here. We are a small but very close-knit family and it is comforting to have their support. Charlie has had heart surgery in the past few years and the sight of Russ refreshes his own memory of hospitals. He leaves the room to sit in the lounge area. Chris explains that he probably feels uncomfortable and I clearly understand why. They leave by late afternoon to return home. Russ has a slightly elevated temperature today of 100.8 so he is put on antibiotics. He moves around quite a bit today, tapping his feet against the footboard. The nurses put him in a cardiac chair, which looks like an oversized chair with thick supports surrounding the head area. He is in the chair for only an hour and I notice that in spite of the thick head cushions, his head droops most of the time. Perhaps this is because of poor muscle tone in the neck but I attempt several times to keep his head somewhat straight.

April 24

The nurses inform us that Russ's temperature is 103 so he is put on additional antibiotics. This worries me but I know that he is in good hands. Russ's son-in- law visits from out of town and I am glad to see him. I've always respected him because he has treated Russ's grandchildren so well, even though they are not his biological children. The trial breathing is going well and Russ continues to cough to rid himself of secretions, which the nurse says is important to prevent pneumonia. As we walk down the hall, I hear my name being called. I turn around to see a co-worker with tears in her eyes. She tells me that her husband has died. We hug each other for a few moments and find comfort in our mutual sorrow. I leave, telling her that I will pray for her and her family during this difficult time. Russ has a long recovery ahead of him but at least he is alive and stable. I feel relieved in this thought but mourn her loss.

April 25

Russ's temperature is now normal again. The nurse explains that he is not considered to be in critical condition anymore so the 9:00am medical team will no longer stop in to evaluate him. Kip and I see this as another sign that he is on the mend. Every day and every improvement confirm his will to survive. Again he is placed in the cardiac chair but as before his neck muscles are weak and he has difficulty supporting his head.

April 26

Today they remove Russ from the ventilator in order to see how he does breathing on his own. A case manager comes in to talk to us about placement in a nursing home/rehabilitation center when he leaves the hospital. She gives me a list of facilities and recommends that we visit any facility we are interested in. The list covers a 40-mile radius from our home. The doctor comes in and instructs Russ to squeeze his hand and wiggle his toes. Russ does not respond to this. The doctor also says that he wants physical therapy to start working with Russ. At mid-afternoon, Russ's grandson and fiancé visit. Russ is becoming more active as he moves his arms around. Kip and I put his arms down so he won't dislodge his tracheotomy but a one point he manages to dislodge it. The nurse notices it and reattaches it. He surprises me by saying, "Let me go, I have to go pee". I tell him to just do it in bed since they have a pad under him. The nurse puts some restraints on him so he won't pull on the tracheotomy again. They have enough slack but not enough to enable him to reach toward his throat. Kip feels her blood pressure rise. I think the day's events and lack of sleep are catching up with her so I take her home where she can rest a bit. Russ is in good hands and I feel I should keep an eye on Kip at home. She lies down for a while as I clean up a little.

April 27

When we arrive at the hospital, they have Russ sitting in the cardiac chair. The nurse explains that they want to get him used to the sitting position and this will help strengthen his muscles. He moves his arms and legs quite a bit, especially his right foot, which he frequently taps. When the doctor arrives, he says that Russ will be moved to a rehab center by the end of the week. He will be consulting Russ's cardiologist to address the problem of the cardiac arrhythmia, which resulted in the cardiac arrest. The nurses return Russ to bed at 9:30am. In the afternoon, 3 physical therapists come to work with him. They manage to sit him up at the side of the bed. While 2 therapists support him on either side, the other one has him dangle his legs over the side of the bed. He quickly falls asleep after they leave.

April 28

As usual, Kip and I arrive at 8am. After an hour, Russ's daughter comes to visit him. I didn't realize that she was in town. She goes to his right side and tries to get his attention by saying" Dad, Dad, don't make me touch your face" Russ doesn't like anyone touching his face. He turns his face away but doesn't say anything. After a few hours, she says that she has some things to do while in town and leaves. I make several phone calls to several nearby nursing homes/rehabilitation centers. After talking to several people and researching them on the Internet, I narrow my list to the top 3. Reputation and distance is important to me. I want the best for Russ and I would like him in a close facility so I can be with him everyday. But after calling the first 2 facilities, I am told that they have no vacancies. Kip and I will visit the 3rd facility, 10 miles away at 11:00 am. The director takes us on a tour and we are impressed by the cleanliness and program. Their physical therapy department consists of many treadmills and other equipment unfamiliar to us. We discuss the possibility of Russ being moved here and the director says she will talk to the hospital social worker about it. This is all so overwhelming and I confess to Kip that this is uncharted territory for me. *Is this the right place for him? Am I doing the best for him?* Kip and I stop for a well-deserved lunch and I take the opportunity to call a well-known rehabilitation center some 50 miles away. I know it's far away but they are supposed to be very good. I call the insurance company first to see if they will cover it. The customer service representative at the insurance company says that the facility is "out of network" and would not be paid for. Since I don't have the money for such an expensive treatment center, I reluctantly cross it off my list. At the hospital the speech therapist and respiratory therapist work to remove his oxygen supplement to see if he can talk more easily. They will install a speaking valve to his tracheotomy to aid in this. A physician's assistant from neurology comes in to see Russ. She calls his name, has him squeeze her hand and wiggle his toes. He responds to her commands. She lets me know that he will be on anti-seizure medicine for a year because of his previous seizure.

April 29

Today a person from respiratory therapy is giving Russ a breathing treatment. Shortly after they leave, a nurse comes in to administer his heparin shot. This is given to prevent blood clots. When the nurse attempts to give him the injection in his abdomen, he pushes her hand away. I move to hold his arms down while she successfully gives him the injection. Later, the nurses get him into the cardiac chair for a few hours. His neck muscles seem to be a little stronger as he is now able to hold his head up better than before. The doctor comes in to report that Russ's vital signs are good. He will talk to the cardiologist about inserting a defibrillator before Russ is released. Later the cardiologist talks to us about options to control the arrhythmia, which caused his cardiac arrest. A mechanical defibrillator would work well but in Russ's precarious condition, it might be a risky move. He prefers medication instead. I agree with this so he will prescribe it upon discharge from the hospital. There are no visitors.

April 30

Our neighbors Dottie and Harlow visit today. They have been visiting Russ every chance they get. Dottie asks Russ if he remembers Harlow and Russ nods yes. She also asks if he's ready to mow the grass, something he always did for them. He shakes his head no. When Kip and I leave for a break, we learn that the doctor visited Russ. I ask the nurse if there is any news to report. She replies that Russ is stable. Russ's gown is undone at his shoulder so Kip asks if he's trying to be sexy to which he shrugs his shoulders. The social worker comes in to tell us that Russ would not be accepted by the rehabilitation center that Kip and I visited because they require patients to undergo 3-hour daily physical therapy sessions. Russ doesn't have the stamina to do this. I wish someone; the rehab center or hospital would have told us about this before we wasted our time visiting the rehab center.

May 1

The doctor comes in to say that Russ is doing very well without the ventilator so they may move him to a regular room. They will re-evaluate which placement he should go to since some facilities are better equipped to treat patients in his condition. He would prefer a facility that concentrates on neurological and cardiac rehabilitation. I will find out later that such facilities are not common. Russ's other sister calls to see how he's doing. There are no visitors today.

May 2

The nurse comes in to give Russ his medication and his daily mouth hygiene with the soft spongy toothbrush and as usual he turns his head from side to side to avoid the task. He will still get a daily visit from a doctor. Russ is down to one IV, his antibiotic. He is receiving his stomach feeding and supplemental oxygen. At midmorning Russ is put in the cardiac chair. I notice that he seems to have better muscle tone in his neck and can now raise his arm plus rub his face with his hand. Kip goes over to his chair and asks him if he loves her. He nods yes. This makes her teary-eyed. The nurse reports that he has far less secretions and continues to cough well to rid him of any he might have. At 2:30, the physical therapists come in to have him again dangle his legs over the side of the bed. He manages to do this with their support. The therapist asks Russ to wave at her, which he does.

May 3

When we arrive this morning, a sports event is on the television. Since Russ could not put it on, we conclude that he must have had a visitor. A case manager comes in to tell us that Russ will be transferred to a skilled nursing home facility where he can recover and receive physical therapy. She hands me a brochure of additional facilities and says I should visit them and asks questions. He will be discharged soon from the hospital and we need to find placement for him. Dottie and Harlow visit at 11:00am. They are good neighbors and friends. I so appreciate their support and concern. In the afternoon, an internist comes in to see Russ. He will order a chest X-ray to make sure that no pneumonia is present. He says that Russ may make a recovery but to prepare myself that he may never fully recover. I know that Russ has a long, difficult recovery ahead of him but I am prepared to take it one day and one victory at a time. I notice that Russ is not very active today. He does not move his arms and tap his feet as he has been doing. I continue to be worried and scared but I realize how important it is to be positive. I cannot give up hope. He is moved to the cardiac chair where he manages to use one foot to remove the blue hospital slipper from the other foot. Then he uses the bar above the remaining foot to remove the other slipper. I ask him if the slippers bother him and he nods "yes". He taps his right foot as if he is keeping the beat to some song.

May 4

As usual, Kip and I arrive at the hospital at 8:30 am. Russ's friend Bill comes into the room at 10:00 am. He volunteers by visiting Catholic patients at the hospital to give them Communion. He was here this morning seeing other patients and wanted to check on Russ. Bill has been a good, loyal friend to us and I appreciate his support. After Bill leaves, the nurse comes in to put his speaking valve in when suddenly Russ tries to bite her hand. I tell him to let her put it in and he replies "no". I explain that this will help him speak better. Finally he agrees to it. The nurse asks him if he's a character to which he answers "sure". Kip tries to get him to say "Kippy". He does so after a few attempts. Russ's other sister visits for a short time in the afternoon. Soon after her departure, he removes the oxygen indicator from his finger. I put it back on his finger and tell him to leave it on. He says "ok". His eyes are open for most of the day. He spends some time again in the cardiac chair. Kip and I visit a nearby nursing home/rehabilitation center. It seems clean and pleasant. We are shown the patient rooms, physical therapy area and the dining area. The weekly menu is posted at the entrance of the dining room along with activities such as movie day and karaoke. This interests Karla since karaoke is her hobby. It's difficult to judge a facility after such a visit but later I look it up on my computer to find no glaring violations or bad reviews. Besides it is close to the house, about 2 miles away. It means I can spend as much time with Russ as possible. This is very important to me and I make the decision to have him recuperate here. Still, in the back of my mind I wonder if I am making the right decision. Later in the evening Kip and I decide we need a break and go to a nearby bar where it is karaoke night. Kip entertains the patrons with several songs. She really is a good singer and much more courageous than I would be in front of strangers. I attempt to enjoy myself but my thoughts are with Russ. *How will he adjust to the nursing home? Is that the best place for him? Will he ever be the man I knew?*

May 5

Two nurses are turning Russ when we arrive at the hospital. He is still unable to do this on his own. The nurses in the cardiac intensive care unit have been amazing. They always inform us of what is going on and answer our many questions. They are patient and compassionate in dealing with Russ. Today they tell us that he again tried to remove his trach. He is breathing very well so the doctor will probably remove it today anyway. Plans for his discharge are in the works, possibly for tomorrow. During the morning, he sleeps most of the time. Three physical therapists come in to again have him sit at the bed's edge. He doesn't cooperate well because of the fatigue, so it takes all three of them to sit him up. It's too bad they didn't come yesterday when he was much more alert. Later the doctor arrives to remove his trach. Russ tolerates this well. All his IV's are gone. The doctor explains that the opening in his throat will quickly close, probably within a week. I find relief in seeing that finally he is not tethered to some machine. The constant rhythmic beeping of the monitor was a reminder that his life was in limbo. Now finally he is breathing on his own. It's something we all do and take for granted. Kip and I take a break in the lounge area. I see the somber faces of people whose loved ones are in crisis. They sit quietly with worried looks on their faces or discuss the situation with family members. I can understand their pain and for a moment want to hug them. I will pray for them instead. When we return to the room, the speech therapist comes in to work with Russ. She asks him if he knows where he's at. He does not reply. She tells him he is in the hospital. He asks "why". Apparently he does not remember what happened. I am grateful for that. She explains that his heart stopped. She also asks him if he works. He replies "part-time". She wants to know what he does at his job. He says "as little as possible". That so sounds like something he would say. He is instructed to hold up 2 fingers, which he does.

May 6

  We learn from the nurse that Russ will be discharged today from the hospital and sent by ambulance to the nursing home. The nurse seems concerned because Russ is lethargic today. She explains that the sedative may play a part in the lethargy. She mentions that I will have to be his advocate since he cannot speak for himself. I didn't realize at this time how prophetic her words would be. The internist comes in to examine Russ and write the discharge orders. I mention to her about his lethargy. She will write an order to gradually decrease the sedatives. He still has his stomach tube and will continue to get the thick oatmeal-colored feedings.

It's a relief to me that all his IV's and breathing apparatus have been discontinued. He is breathing well on his own. However, he is still very weak and dependent. Russ's sister and son come in at mid-morning. Bill also visits. I thank all the nurses for their hard work. Last evening, Kip and I bought them a gift basket containing fruit, cheese and crackers. I feel fortunate that Russ has received a very high standard of care here. However I worry that the nursing home will not have such high standards.

The ambulance finally arrives at noon to transport Russ to the nursing home. Kip and I follow in the car. When we arrive at the nursing home, we announce ourselves at the nursing station, which is a circular structure near the entrance. Four resident wings fan out from there. Russ has been taken to the A wing. He is sharing a room with another resident who sits watching an episode of Gunsmoke on the television. Russ's bed is really too short for his 6' 0" frame and his ankles and feet hang over the footboard. I notice that there are no bedrails. The LPN attempts to connect his bag of stomach feeding but has trouble with it. She goes to get another device that finally works. The feeding is in a plastic bag similar to an IV bag and the machine pumps the feeding through a long tube directly into his stomach. The opening is on his torso with the tube protruding from the opening. A dressing secures the tube. The nurse tells us that the social worker wants me to go to her office. I have papers to sign, she explains. She wonders if I have power of attorney. I tell her no. Russ and I never talked about this and now I regret that we didn't. We were busy living our lives and never expected a catastrophic illness, especially one that happened so suddenly. She says that Russ will have to sign one of the papers. I look at her with a shocked look on my face. There is a moment of silence before I tell her that he is barely out of a coma with very limited physical and cognitive abilities. There is no way he could sign anything. Has she even seen him? Does she know the limitations of a brain injury? This does not impress me at all. She needs to actually see the patient before she makes such a ridiculous request. This does little to ease my mind about the kind of care Russ will get here. We stay with Russ until early evening and return home to have supper. At 9:30pm, I get a call from the nursing home that Russ is vomiting and has diarrhea. He is sent back to the hospital for evaluation. We are back again in the Emergency Room where he is given medication to control his problems.   When he is stable, he is sent back to the nursing home. We stay with him until 1:30am and then return home. At 3:00am we get a call that he pulled the stomach tube out so he's back at the hospital to have it reattached. Although I am exhausted I return once more to the Emergency Room where they quickly reattach the stomach tube. At dawn I return home to finally get some much needed sleep.

May 7

   In the morning Kip and I visit Russ to find that his bed has been lowered, almost to the floor. There is a mattress on the floor next to the bed. The nurse reports that he had a restless night and was rolling around so they put the mattress on the floor in case he managed to roll out of bed. I ask her about the lack of bedrails. She explains that bedrails are not allowed because of state regulations. Physical restraints are in this category of what is forbidden. After we return from lunch, we find out that Russ again dislodged his stomach tube and was taken back to the hospital to reinsert it. After 3 hours he returns to the nursing home. This time the doctor has sutured the area around the tube so he can't remove it. Russ is still agitated and moves around. Kip and I try to calm him down. This is a different environment than the hospital and I believe he is having trouble adjusting to it. He really doesn't understand what is going on despite our efforts to alleviate his fears. Hopefully this is a minor setback. As always I try to stay positive. Stephanie calls and I tell her about the day's activities.

May 8

This is another restless day for Russ. He is in a cardiac chair. It's not as sophisticated as the one in the hospital but is a larger, more cushioned version of a wheelchair. Noticeable bruises are on the entire length of his left and right legs. These are on both arms also. I am appalled by it all. It looks as if he has been a loser in a fight. I confront a nurse about this and she explains that he was very restless last night, kicking the wall or any other fixed structure in his way. The staff put him in the chair so he wouldn't harm himself anymore. Kip and I again try to calm him down and after a short while, he falls asleep. Yesterday I brought some clothes for him to wear. He has his own closet in the room with a sign on the door indicating that I will do his laundry. I don't want to take the chance of any clothes being misplaced by their laundry department. I notice that he only has a T-shirt and his briefs on. Although I brought pants for him, they are not on him. This angers me since he is out in the hallway without any pants on. Could they at least maintain some of his dignity by having him fully dressed? He has been through enough without this. I go to the director's office I talk to the nursing director about this. I want his pants on when he is in the hall. Russ continues to be agitated and moves his arms and legs constantly. He kicks his legs out and I make sure that nothing is in his way. He is biting his lip so hard that blood appears. I take a washcloth and wipe the blood from it. I talk to him in a quiet reassuring voice telling him that everything will be ok and that he should take it easy. The nurse comes in to administer his medication directly into his stomach tube. Finally, overcome with exhaustion Russ is returned to bed and falls asleep.

May 9

I arrive in the morning to find Russ in the hall again in a T-shirt and briefs. A nurse is in the hall dispensing medication and I confront her about this oversight. She pauses to talk. I express my concern about the briefs. She tells me that she put this request in his chart. I hope it isn't the beginning of further problems at this facility. I will definitely watch them carefully. I want Russ to have great care especially after all he's been through. Russ's roommate is a nice man who seems mentally sharp but has mobility issues. He tells me he is from Chicago and since I am too, we talk about the changes in the city. He warns me to watch the staff here and to carefully read anything they want me to sign.

May 10

At 8:30 I am in Russ's room where this time, he only has his briefs on. Before I have the chance to complain, an aide comes in to say he has just had a bath and she just now had the time to get him dressed. This facility seems to be understaffed and the aides, especially, are overwhelmed. Russ is really tired today. While Kip and I are out to lunch, the doctor comes to see Russ. I ask the nurse if he had anything to report. She only says that he ordered an additional sedative because of his agitation. For now, I will not contest this. But as Russ improves, I will monitor it.

May 11

The doctor visits again today while I am there. I ask him about the sedatives and how long Russ will have to take them. He replies that the nurses will observe him to see how he improves. Then the dosage will be gradually decreased based on his behavior. Russ is somewhat more responsive today although he has bitten his lip so I get a wet washcloth to wipe the blood off. I then apply Vaseline to his lips that are very dry. A cheerful man with black hair and round face comes in to tell us that he is the physical therapist. He will have Russ dangle his legs over the side of the bed. He calls Russ's name loudly and helps him to sit up. He moves his legs to the bed's side and supports Russ while his legs dangle. The physical therapist praises Russ for his efforts. I notice that Russ's arm movements are more controlled, not like the erratic ones I observed in the past week. He has more control over all his limbs. The past few days were a tough adjustment for him. Hopefully things will get better now. At home, I do research on cardiac arrest on the Internet and learn that 40,000 people die every year in auto accidents, 30,000 people die every year from breast or prostrate cancer while 325,000 die every year from cardiac arrest. Less than 10% of cardiac arrest victims survive. Russ may have a long, difficult recovery but at least he is in the minority that survived the devastating cardiac arrest. I am so grateful that he is still in my life.

May 12

We are greeted this morning by the physical therapist who is in Russ's room to work on some exercises. The therapist takes Russ's arm and slowly starts to rotate it. After a few arm exercises, he takes Russ's leg, bends it and stretches it. He explains that this will strengthen his limbs so they can do more complex tasks, which will eventually lead to walking. The nurse comes in to change Russ's feeding container. The container is just about empty. She said that he tried to again remove his stomach tube but she managed to stop him. We have had several nightly calls from the nursing home telling us that he was taken to the hospital to have the stomach tube reinserted after he dislodged it. They cannot use any restraints on his arms so he has removed the tube on occasion. By early afternoon, the nurse announces that they will move Russ to a private room closer to the nurses' station so they can keep a closer watch on him. By the time we return from lunch Russ is in his new room. It is a bigger room and has enough space so Kip and I can sit with space to spare. I have been bringing a folding chair from home since there is only one chair in each room for visitors. Although Russ was sleepy in the morning, he is now more alert and tries to reposition himself in bed. These beds are still short for his 6'0" frame but they are the only beds that the facility has. He rests his feet on the footboard. Later he tries to remove his shorts and briefs. When I look closer I realize that he needs clean briefs. Although he doesn't verbalize it, I think he felt the wetness and attempted to do something about it. He has several visitors today including Bill plus our neighbors Dottie and Harlow.

May 13

We notice that Russ is quite drowsy today so we quietly keep him company. The nurse adjusts his tube feeding since it stopped because of a misfed line. As we leave for lunch, Russ's sister and ex-wife greet us in the parking lot. His sister asks if his ex-wife can see him. I agree without hesitation. They were married for quite a few years and had three children together. She has every right to see him. Later, Russ's niece and her young son visit. He is quite curious about the tube feeding and examines it carefully. His mother explains what it is for and why it's needed. She reminisces about how Russ would tease and play tricks on her constantly when she was a child. He even put on top of a refrigerator and left her there until she protested so loudly that he finally returned her to the floor. Before they leave, she wants her son to touch Russ's hand. He is reluctant to do so. I tell her that perhaps it's not a good idea to make him do it. Russ is still very sick and looks it. I can imagine that the sight of him could be frightening for a young child.

May 14

Russ is again quite drowsy and sleeps most of the morning. By afternoon he is more alert. He attempts to remove his gown and I tell him to keep it on. Kip asks him if he's trying to impress the nurse. He shrugs his shoulders in response. I notice that the skin on his feet is dry and cracked so I ask him if he wants me to rub lotion on them. He replies "no". I will try later. He says in his new raspy deep voice that he is hot. The voice is not like his usual one and I believe it's this way because of the tracheotomy so I am hopeful it will return to normal soon. Although the nursing home has air conditioning, it is most effective near the entrance and nurses station. The patient wings are somewhat stuffy and warm. I have brought a box fan from home that I labeled with his name. I do not want it to "disappear". I'm glad I did bring it and now turn the dial to high. An aide comes in to take Russ's temperature but he moves his head from side to side to avoid the thermometer so she puts it in his armpit. He finally lets me rub some lotion on his feet and I do so while massaging them. Before we leave, Kip asks him if she can kiss his head. He agrees to this. She kisses his forehead and tells him that she loves him. She will be returning to California tomorrow. I am happy to see the progress he has made so far. Something like him scratching his foot with his hand or rubbing his beard. These seem like ordinary movements that we take for granted but for Russ they are another victory.

May 15

I drop Kip off at the airport at 8:00am for her 10:00am flight home. We hug each other after I help her unload her luggage. I thank her for all the support she's given to Russ and me. I don't know what I would have done without her. She has become more than a sister-in-law, she's become a good friend. I know that she feels some comfort in realizing that Russ survived the worst medical crisis of his life. She has seen him emerge from a critical condition, dependent on a ventilator, unable to speak or breath on his own and then finally able to speak. I feel very alone on the ride back to the nursing home. *Am I equipped for all the challenges that lie ahead of me? I have to because Russ is depending on me.* Russ is sleeping when I get to the nursing home. His bed is in the lowest position with the mattress next to it in case he propels his way to the floor. Next to the mattress is a long bumper pad to prevent injury. Their options are limited because of state regulations.

May 16

This morning I tell Russ good morning when I get to the nursing home at 9:00am. He turns his head in response. The nurse comes in to give him his morning medications. She asks where he had worked and he tells her he worked in a factory. He did work as a forklift driver some years ago at a factory. Later when the aide comes in to take his temperature, again he moves his head from side to side, preventing her from taking it. I tell him to keep still so she can take it. To my surprise, he allows her to take it. After she leaves he smiles in his quirky way. He can be quite a jokester and I realize he was just being himself at her expense. He wipes his nose with his hand so I ask him if he'd like a tissue. He says yes but when I give it to him, he opens his mouth and clicks his teeth like he's going to bite me. He's in a playful mood but I tell him to behave himself. He's smiling that way again.

May 17

I arrive this morning to find the aides positioning a blue sling under Russ. They gather the attached hooks and move a large machine over the bed. After attaching the hooks to the machine they flip a switch that picks Russ up and lowers him into the specialized chair. They say that he is going to physical therapy. I go along with him. There the therapist throws a large balloon to Russ and instructs him to catch it. Russ does a good job catching most of the balloon tosses. The therapist then pushes Russ's chair to the end of the parallel bars where he instructs him to get up and stand between the parallel bars. Russ slowly rises and stands, all the time holding onto the bars. The therapist stands nearby to spot him. Russ stands for 2 minutes before returning to the chair. What a milestone! A little over a month ago, he was in a coma, unable to breathe on his own, tethered to an array of IV's and now he is taking a few steps. I desperately needed some good events in my life. This great accomplishment energizes me. I will call Kip when I get home to tell her the good news.

May 18

Although Russ's room has a television, I have not had the need to turn it on. But when I arrived today, it was tuned into a music channel. The sound emitting from it was hip-hop. I searched for an oldies station instead since I thought Russ would like it better. I never thought about having a music station playing but now I think it might be a good distraction for him and me. Sure enough, after I put the station on, Russ is keeping the beat by moving his left arm up and down to the song "Nowhere To Run". I ask him if he is rocking and rolling. He replies "yes".

May 19

Today Russ is in bed with only his briefs on. I ask the nurse about this and am told he complained about being hot. I also learn that he again removed his stomach tube that prompted a ride to the hospital to have it reattached. This time they have put a wide binder around his torso. It is secured with Velcro so hopefully he won't bother it. He sleeps most of the morning, changing positions from sleeping on his back to rolling onto his side. He is getting stronger in his movements. One of our neighbors, Roxanne, comes in later to visit him where she finds him asleep. Later the physical therapist comes in to have Russ sit at the edge of the bed. He tells Russ to stand up close to the walker the therapist brought in. Russ holds onto the walker and takes a few steps. He bounces up and down to the beat of the music channel. After getting Russ in the chair, the therapist instructs Russ to comb his hair. He has given him a comb and Russ manages to comb his own hair.

May 20

Russ is drowsy in the morning but is more alert in the afternoon. I hold his hand for a while. He puts my hand close to his mouth. I am thinking that he will attempt to bite it, but instead he gently kisses it. Our friend Bill and his daughter Jenny visit Russ. Bill asks Russ how he is to which Russ replies "sick". Later in the day, Russ's niece and her son come to visit. Her son finds a balloon in the room and starts to throw it around. At 3:00pm I leave the nursing home. My daily routine consists of arriving there at 8:00am and leaving at 3:00pm. This leaves me time to do some work at home. Today I will go to the supermarket and then to the home improvement store to get flowers plus mulch. When I get home I spread the mulch around the flowerbeds and plant some of the purchased flowers. I need some normalcy in my life and this task is a step in that direction. When I finish, I check my Facebook page. Last month I kept family and friends aware of Russ's condition and asked for prayers. I continue to update them of his progress. I follow their lives: going camping or on vacation, having lunch with friends, attending graduations or weddings. This used to be my life, my normalcy. But now normalcy means the cycle of staying at the nursing home 6-7 hrs a day, coming home to do chores and crying before I fall asleep. I miss my previous normal life but realize that I must be positive but realistic about Russ's recovery. He has suffered brain damage. Time will tell to what extent. At least that's what the doctors have told me. They are vague when asked about his prognosis. I suppose they don't want to give people false hope. I continue to ask God for strength to get me through this.

May 21

Today the nurse informed me that Russ again pulled his stomach tube out so he went to the hospital. This is becoming a common occurrence still I wish he would leave it alone. I suppose that the stomach tube is an irritant to him and he wants to get rid of it. He doesn't realize that it is his present nourishment, keeping him alive. Later on, he attempts to remove the stomach tube again so the doctor orders an additional temporary sedative. This lulls him into sleep for the entire time I am there.

Some friends visit the now sleeping Russ. Today he is not good company.

May 22

Russ is in the chair when I arrive. He is awake and I notice that his hair is awry. I offer him the comb. He needs to take small steps to self-help skills and combing his own hair is a start in the right direction. The end result is not perfect but he has done a commendable job to a neater appearance. The nurse comes in to give him his tube feeding and states that he is calmer today. For the time being, he has left the stomach tube intact. The binder must be uncomfortable though. The aide takes his blood pressure and pulse later in the afternoon. She tells me that Russ was joking with her yesterday. I have read how patient personalities can change after a brain injury. Russ has maintained his somewhat mischievous personality and even his favorite sayings, "Russisms" I call them.

May 23

Russ is awake and alert this morning. Our friend, Bill visits and asks Russ if he is ready to play golf, his favorite game. Russ says "ok". When the nurse comes in to give Russ his medications and tube feeding, he puts his hand on her shoulder. He is reaching for the binder to remove it. I quickly intervene and tell him to leave it alone. He does so, at least for now. The director of nursing comes in to announce that they will have a speech therapist start to work with Russ in an attempt to have him eat solid food. The therapist is very busy so it might be a few days before she sees him. What an exciting prospect, to have him eat! This is one more step in his amazing recovery. He still has a long difficult road ahead of him but nevertheless I am thrilled with this small victory.

May 24

Russ looks quite peaceful in his sleep this morning. Another resident comes in with her walker and asks me how her "sweetie" is doing. Her inviting smile and friendly disposition put me at ease. She tells me her name. Her white hair and deep wrinkles lead me to believe that she is in her early 80's. There is an excitement in her voice as she tells me that today the hair stylist will be doing her hair today. It sounds like she's looking forward to it. Women of all ages want to look their best. She says she stops in to check on Russ during her daily walks. I thank her for her concern. Later, the aides use the mechanical lift to position Russ in his chair. Dottie and Harlow visit. Dottie asks Russ if he remembers her. He nods "yes". But when asked if he remembers Harlow, he wrinkles his forehead as if struggling to think about it. He does not reply. I give him the comb so he can smooth his hair. As I reach to get the comb, he pulls my head toward him and kisses my forehead. No words are exchanged but the feelings are clear. Our love for each other is even stronger now. At 2:30 the physical therapist comes in to bring Russ to the physical therapy room. The therapist puts a gait belt on Russ. This is a special cloth belt put around the waist to steady the patient. It can also be grabbed quickly if the patient starts to fall. With the therapist at Russ's side and me following with the chair, Russ is instructed to walk as far as he can. He walks 50 feet and then turns around to walk back another 50 feet.

When his pace quickens, the therapist reminds him to slow down. The therapist praises Russ for doing so well. After Russ is returned to his room, he soon closes his eyes and sleeps. The walk must have tired him out. A walk that so many of us could do easily is a tremendous effort for Russ, 6 weeks post cardiac arrest.

May 25

When I arrive at 9:00 am, I find Russ's binder undone and although his stomach tube is still attached, its contents are leaking onto his sheet. I find an aide to tell her about it. She says she will return shortly to change the bed linens. After 45 minutes during which I look out in the hallway for any aide, someone finally comes in to change the linens and correct the leaking tube. She apologizes saying that many aides were attending an in-service and were just now trying to catch up on their tasks. She says that yesterday she got Russ to sit up at the edge of the bed and walk a few steps to his chair. They didn't need to use the mechanical sling. She gets him now to brush his teeth and comb his hair. She wants him to learn self-help skills and I agree with her. I attend a care conference later for Russ. This is required by the state. The social worker, occupational therapist and director of nursing are in attendance. Since the first meeting with the social worker didn't impress me, I'm not thrilled to see her. The director of nursing wants to know if I have any concerns or questions. I mention that I would really like to see him in bed at night and in the chair during the daytime. There have been instances where he has been in the chair all day and all night. I also express my concern about the high dosage of sedatives he is on. They need to start weaning him off these medications. The director says she will talk to the doctor about this. As usual I return to our empty house and busy myself with weeding and watering the flower garden. I get ready for bed, a bed that seems so lonely without Russ. I always felt safe with him at my side. Now I make sure that both front and back doors are securely locked. As I am washing my face, I get a call from the nursing home saying that Russ once again pulled out his stomach tube and is on his way to the hospital to have them reattach it. The first few times this happened, I rushed to the hospital emergency room but now it seems so routine, I don't bother. The hospital staff have him back at the nursing home in a short time, so it's not worth my effort. I wish the staff at the nursing home could reattach it themselves. I am also angry with Russ for pulling it out. I've talked to him about this but I don't think he comprehends what he's doing.

May 26

This morning Russ is lying on the mattress next to his bed. I am told that he rolled onto it during the night. Two aides come in shortly to help him into his chair. He is able now to stand on his own and walk a little. Therefore they do not need the mechanical lift anymore. The tall aide with her black hair in a tight ponytail gives Russ a comb and instructs him to comb his hair. He slowly and carefully runs the comb through his hair until it is neatly done. She now gives him a toothbrush, a glass of water and a basin so he can brush his teeth. He does this successfully. It's good to see him do these small tasks on his own. By early afternoon, Russ is taken to physical therapy. The therapist walks beside him as he walks the entire length of the room and back to his chair. After this, Russ is returned to the chair where he, the physical therapist and I throw a large ball to each other. Russ is able to catch and throw the ball with ease. He is taken over to a machine where his feet are placed onto pedals and his hands are placed onto handles. It reminds me of a modified stationary bike. The therapist encourages Russ to pedal with his feet and hold onto the handles that make circular motions when rotated. Russ gets fatigued but the therapist wants him to do a few more so I tell him that he can do it. After all the exercise he easily falls fast asleep.

May 27

This morning the scowl on Russ's face tells me that he may not be in the greatest mood. When I touch his hand, he pulls it away. I decide that it's best to give him his distance so I sit in the chair without talking. We listen to the oldies playing on the television music channel. Later in the morning, Bill visits and says hello to Russ. Bill extends his hand to have Russ shake it. Russ shakes his hand and asks how he is doing. I think he recognizes Bill since he asks Bill if he brought Buster, the dog, with him. Shortly before noon, the speech therapist comes in with a tray containing small cups of various liquids. She will have Russ taste the liquids and watch how well he swallows them. The first liquid she tries is apple juice thickened with a powder. This makes it easier to swallow, she explains. As he drinks the apple juice, she watches his throat for proper swallowing. He does this easily without coughing or gagging. She next tries some thickened coffee and finally cranberry juice. Russ makes a face and says he doesn't like the cranberry juice. Next, she gives him pureed mashed potatoes, which goes down easily. The last food she tries is softened meat. Russ has some trouble with this since it has more substance and has to be chewed. She gives him water to aid his swallowing. She will leave him sitting upright in the chair for a few minutes so he doesn't have any problems with choking. They will start him now on pureed foods, then soft foods and eventually regular food. All of this is to take place in the next few weeks.

May 28

I arrive at the nursing home early at 8:00 am. I want to see Russ before I have to leave to pick up Stephanie, my son-in-law Neil and granddaughter Karina at the airport. They are coming here to visit me and at last I'll get to see my granddaughter for the first time. She is now 6 weeks old and has the dark eyes of her father and the sweet face of her mother. I was scheduled to fly to Virginia in April shortly after her birth but the events of April 11 changed that. Now I will get to see her and I can't wait. Russ is sleeping the entire time I'm here. At 9:30 I leave for the airport, a 45-minute drive from here. Their flight arrives and I am anxiously waiting for a glimpse of them. Other passengers pass by me and are greeted by loved ones. It seems like an eternity but finally I see a couple with a stroller. It's Stephanie, Neil and Karina. I kneel down to see Karina who looks like a beautiful little angel. She squirms and makes a tiny baby noise. Stephanie says she did well on the flight, sleeping most of the time. After Karina is buckled into the car seat, we depart for home. My sister Chris and brother-in-law Charlie are making the 3-hour drive today to see us. It is so good to have my family here. Although our family is small compared to other families, we are close and have always been supportive of one another. When they arrive, we all go to see Russ who is sleeping again. Neil and Karina stay outside the nursing home on a bench. A nursing home and its possible germs are no place for such a young child. When the aides come in to clean Russ up, we all walk down the hall to visit Russ's former roommate. He talks about his past and how he was in a band. One of his first jobs was delivering ice for customers' iceboxes. It's very easy to hear him talk about his life. I don't think he gets many visitors so I'm glad we could talk with him. After a few hours we go to the house where we enjoy some supper. Chris and Charlie take off for their home. How great it was to have them visit.

May 29
    We are at the nursing home at 9:00am and find a planter of yellow chrysanthemums on the windowsill. A friend, Audrey, has sent them. The sunny yellow color brightens the otherwise drab room. Later another friend of ours brings a do-it-yourself kit containing marigold seeds and a planter. Since it is Memorial Day weekend, Stephanie has invited some friends and relatives to the house. I will leave the entertaining to Stephanie since she's much better at it than I am. At 10:30am my niece, her children and grandma arrive. Soon afterward, we all proceed to an upscale restaurant for lunch. Stephanie went to the store yesterday and purchased some meat, cheese and lettuce to make wraps along with fruit and

vegetables. I help her arrange these on the table, buffet style. At mid-afternoon her high school friends come in. She has not seen them in a while and they renew their friendships by hugging. Everyone admires Karina for the short time she is awake. 14 visitors. I've never had that many people in our house before. It's a little overwhelming. The dark sky tells of an impending storm. Soon the wail of a siren alerts us of a tornado warning. All these people and we don't have a basement. I can tell that Stephanie is getting worried for Karina's well being. I turn on the television to see where the tornado was spotted. I am relieved that it is south of here moving east, away from us. We do encounter some heavy rain but it is over in a few minutes. We can now relax and eat. Karina has received many gifts of clothing and toys from the guests. By 6:30pm all the guests have departed so I return to the nursing home for a few hours while Stephanie cleans up.

May 30

   I am back at the nursing home early in the morning to see Russ, who is awake. I ask him how he's doing to which he answers "ok". Just before noon, I return back home since Neil's parents and brother have arrived. They had a 2-hour drive and are hungry so we all go to a nearby chain restaurant. They want to see how Russ is doing. We all go to his room but find that he is not there. The nurse tells us that he is in physical therapy. We find him in his chair tossing a ball to the therapist. She returns it to him. He successfully catches it many times. The therapist now gets him out of the chair and has him walk by himself across the room. He quickens his pace so she reminds him to slow down a little. Neil's parents are impressed with his progress. We all return home where we watch Karina hold a small stuffed animal. She is lying on a blanket making baby noises. Shortly before sunset, Neil's family leaves for home. It was good to see them. An hour later the nursing home calls to say that Russ managed to get out of his chair and has fallen. He is not hurt but they have moved him out in the hallway close to the nurse's station to keep a closer watch on him. I go to the nursing home to see for myself if he is indeed ok. I tell him that it's important to stay in the chair and ask for assistance.

May 31
   I arrive at the nursing home early today because Stephanie, Neil and Karina will need a ride to the airport. It's been great having them here but they must return home. Russ is in bed and says his feet are cold so I get a blanket from the closet to cover his feet. Stephanie comes in mid-morning after getting me a Skype camera along with a plant for Russ's room. An hour later she says good-bye to Russ and we leave for the airport. I tearfully hug Stephanie and Neil. I give Karina a kiss on the cheek. I will really miss her. On the way home it hits me that I am alone again, a feeling I don't like. After stopping for lunch, I proceed to the nursing home. The occupational therapist is working with Russ on some self-help skills. She has him lather and shave his face. He does well, although he gets some lather on his ear. After slowly shaving his face, the therapist notices some spots that he has missed and helps him correct them. She instructs him to comb his hair. Just before 6pm I return to an empty house. I find some leftover wraps and salad for dinner.

June 1

It's a quiet morning at the nursing home since Russ is sleeping all morning. Another resident peeks in to ask how her "sweetie" is doing. I take the bag of dirty laundry home with me as I leave to get some lunch. When I return Russ drinks some apple juice and water under the watchful eye of the physical therapist. She again watches his throat as he swallows. Next she has him try some mashed potatoes and even part of a muffin. He easily swallows these without choking. She says how pleased she is with his progress. It's amazing how well he's doing considering that less when 2 months ago he was barely alive, connected to numerous IVs and other life sustaining machines. The occupational therapist then comes in to have him hold a small weight in his hand. She has him bend his arm 10 times then puts the weight in his other hand and has him bend this arm 10 times. When she tells him to raise his arm with the weight in it, he says he's tired but she encourages him to do as much as he can. He successfully does the exercises but rests afterwards. The activity has fatigued him. Our neighbors Harlow and Dottie visit, along with Don and another couple who have become friendly with us. Whenever we've had potluck dinners at the clubhouse, they call to make sure they sit near us.

June 2

Russ is somewhat more awake and alert today. At 10:00am he starts to squirm around and says, "I have to pee" so I find a urinal. After helping him undo his shorts and briefs, I position the urinal to he can use it. I empty the urinal in the bathroom and find the nurse to tell her that he has successfully used the urinal. This is a great step forward for him but I know that it will only happen if I am present. The nursing home doesn't have the staff to monitor him in a timely manner. There is a call button so I will attempt to teach Russ to use it when he feels he has to urinate. I clip the call button to his sheet so he can easily reach it. I show him how to use it to summon help. Hopefully he will understand my instructions. His short- term memory is very poor since the cardiac arrest and he quickly forgets instructions that are given to him.

June 3

When I arrive, I find that Russ is in bed with the sheet covering the entire length of his body including over his face. I take the sheet away from his face. He moves a little in response to this. About an hour later the occupational therapist comes in and adjusts the bed into a sitting position. She has a weight in her hand. She holds it out in front of her and tells Russ to reach for it. He does this easily. She now holds the weight at various distances, at the left and right side, above her and below. Russ is able to follow her movements to get the weight. The aides come in later to move him into the chair. The speech therapist comes in with a tray containing tator tots, cole slaw, fish and mixed fruit. He eats everything except for the fish. He never did like fish. The therapist is pleased with his chewing and swallowing abilities. Bill stops in to say hello. I'm not sure Russ recognizes him but he seems happy to see him. Later one of the aides stops in to see how he is doing. He says hello to her and reaches out with both arms to give her a hug. Today is a good day.

June 4

I usually have the oldies radio station on for Russ but today I thought I'd switch things up so I tune in a country station instead. He is also a country music fan. Tim McGraw's "One, Two, Three Like A Bird I Sing" is playing and soon Russ is singing along with the chorus. He remembers every word. Harlow and Dottie visit. Again Russ remembers Dottie but not Harlow. They tell us that they are going to their favorite vacation spot, Myrtle Beach, South Carolina. I tell them to have a great time and Russ waves good-bye to them as they leave. Shortly after noon, Russ's daughter, son-in-law and grandchildren visit. The girls have colored some pictures for him. I tape these to his closet door. I leave at 3:00pm to do some chores but three hours later am interrupted by a call from the nursing home saying that Russ managed to undo the straps that securely keep him in his chair. He rose to get out of the chair and fell on his face. They will take facial X-rays to make sure no bones are broken. I rush back to the nursing home to find Russ in the hallway near the nurses' station. He has an inch long scrape on his nose. Thankfully, no bones are broken. The staff moves him back to his room to rest. I stay with him for a while and tell him not to undo the straps. I don't know how well he'll listen to me. Before I leave, I position the mattress in front of his chair as a precaution.

June 5

Russ rests for much of the day. I turn the oldies station on and when Roy Orbeson's "Only The Lonely" plays, Russ surprises me by singing along to the tune. He correctly remembers the lyrics and I soon join him in singing. The oldies station helps pass the time and is useful therapy for him. It's amazing that he can sing along to the lyrics but does not remember what day, year it is or how old he is. Later, his daughter, son-in-law and grandchildren visit again. She tells Russ that she loves him and hugs him. This brings a tear to his eye. His son and grandson also visit. We get a pillow from the closet to put behind Russ's back since he says his back is hurting. I am grateful for the visitors that have come to see how he is and to show their support.

June 6

I arrive at the nursing home at 6:00am to spend the next hour with Russ. Today I must return to work since my family leave is done. I will stay with him until 7:00am when I have to leave for work. I will be back after work at 2:45pm and stay with him until 3:45pm before I leave for my second job. At 8:15pm I'll return for a half hour to check on him. It's a strenuous schedule but only for a short time. The school year will end in a few weeks so things will be less hectic for a while. I am fortunate to have the two jobs. They enable us to pay all the bills. There is guilt in leaving him here for so many hours but soon I'll be able to be with him for the majority of the day.

June 7

This is another day of running between my jobs, home and the nursing home. Russ is in the chair positioned out in the hall near the nurses' station. The nurse tells me that he does better out in the hall where he can see the staff passing by and observe other patients who are near the nurses' station. This is a better situation for him instead of being isolated in his room. Several staff members say hello to him as they go about their daily tasks. They stop for a moment to ask him how he is doing. He replies "ok". I kiss him on the forehead and add that I love him before I go to work.

June 8

When I arrive at 2:45pm, I learn that Russ is in the physical therapy room so I make my way down the long hall that leads to the therapy room. He is walking unassisted but with therapists on both sides of him. His gait is steadier today. The therapist says that he was on the modified stationary bike earlier and did well. I am happy with the progress I've seen in his motor skills.

June 9

This afternoon, Russ is sitting in the hall. I get a chair from his room and put it beside him so I can keep him company. There are residents all around the nurses' station, some in wheelchairs or in specialized chairs. I watch them trying to assess what condition they are in. One man who appears to be in his early 50s is in an almost prone position. Only his eyes move and then just a little. This previously handsome, perhaps vital man now lies unable to do even the most basic tasks. A woman, possibly in her 50's, sits more upright in one of the specialized chairs. Her head is tilted to one side while she constantly kicks her right leg against the leg rest. She makes an attempt to speak but only garbled, incomprehensible sounds are heard. I realize that Russ is indeed fortunate to have the skills that he has. Even though he has much work ahead of him, he can communicate and do some self-help tasks. When I return the chair to his room, I notice a back and white cat ambling down the hall. I bend down to pet it and it rubs its side against my leg. This small animal brings some joy into this dreary place.

June 10

Soon after I arrive at the nursing home, the social worker finds me. She wants to talk to me about something, so we sit in the lobby. I am informed that the insurance will only pay for 3 more weeks of physical therapy so Russ will then be discharged from the nursing home. My first question is why, since he is making such good progress. She explains that he has "plateaued". According to this definition, he is not progressing. I vehemently disagree but she makes a point of saying that they have written criteria. I ask to see this written criteria. We go to the physical therapy office where I am shown these documents. Indeed, the wording seems deceptive but basically says that although Russ can walk a certain distance and perform certain exercises, his progress is stalled at these tasks. I explain that surely the more advanced tasks will take time, especially considering what he's been through. But they stick to their interpretation of the standards. I leave to call the case manager at the insurance company. Hopefully I can fight this. The case manager insists that the insurance company will only pay for the 3 more weeks of therapy. I am learning the hard way about the limitations the insurance companies put on certain medical therapies. I depart the nursing home feeling angry and disappointed.

June 11

Russ is once again out in the hall with a gown on but his brief exposed so I find a sheet in the closet to cover him up. The nurse comes to ask if I am staying for a while. He can be in the room as long as I stay with him. They are afraid they he will manage to get out of the chair and hurt himself. She pushes the chair into his room. She lifts his left shoulder to straighten it out. He winces in response to this action so she asks if his shoulder hurts. He replies "yes". She notices that the pad under his shoulder has slipped out of place leaving the shoulder on the metal. After repositioning the pad, she returns with pain medication for him. Later in the afternoon, I am surprised to see a physical therapist come to get Russ for a session. I didn't think they had any therapists who worked on the weekends. Because the therapist is the only one there this weekend, he explains that he cannot have Russ walk. But back in the physical therapy room, he has Russ do 2 sets of 10 leg raises from the chair. Then he raises his legs from the knee. He has him catch a medium-sized ball thrown from different angles. Shortly after 4:00pm, I leave to mow the grass and catch up on other chores.

June 12

I find the nurse giving Russ his medication into the stomach tube. Hopefully they can remove it soon. He is awake and alert for this but soon falls asleep. It is now 8:00am and it isn't until 11:15am that anyone checks on him. By then an aide comes in to wash and change him. He lifts his hips to assist her with the brief change. She moves him to the chair. I leave during the late afternoon. I tell Russ that I will see him later to which he replies, " If you're lucky". That is something he always used to say. I am grateful to hear it.

June 13

   At 6:00am I arrive at the nursing home to find Russ sitting in the hallway, as usual. This time though, he is awake and alert. I tell him that I am glad to see him this way. I ask him if he slept well last night to which he replies "no". I quiz him on what day it is but again the sense of time eludes him as he answers incorrectly. He then gently takes my hand and holds it. It's a simple gesture but one that means the world to me especially since we both have been through a kind of hell, him a physical one and me an emotional one. We continue to hold hands and enjoy this quiet affirmation of our love. When I return at 2:50pm I find him still in the hallway, awake. At least he can observe the staff rushing to their duties and the other residents surrounding the nurses' station. I ask him if he's had physical therapy. He has not, according to him.   Then I ask if the speech therapist had him eat some food. He tells me that she had him eat beans and some "white stuff". He then tells me that he has to go the 5th floor. I tell him that there is only 1 floor to this building. Obviously this is another example of his mental confusion. He then announces that he has to go pee. I push him back to his room where I close the curtain and give him the urinal. Afterwards, I empty it and wash my hands. I know that this is the only time he uses the urinal even though I've taught him how to use the call button. He forgets the instructions and has to rely on the staff that are too busy with their many residents.

June 14

This morning Russ is in the hallway but is obviously drowsier today so I just pull up a chair and sit next to him. Even though my time with him recently has been limited because of my 2 jobs, I cherish any time we spend together. Before I leave I water the plants on his windowsill and open the blinds. I am finishing my last week of school before summer break. It's been an extremely difficult schedule but I only have 4 more days until I can again enjoy his company.

June 15

Russ is still drowsy this morning but more awake when I get there in the afternoon. The petite, gray-haired resident stops by his chair to ask how her "sweetie" is, referring to Russ. I notice that she likes to wander the halls supported by her walker and talks to the other residents. Russ replies "fine" to her inquiry. I stop by the auto repair garage where I ask about the status of our SUV. I brought it in earlier because it vibrated when I stepped on the brakes. The mechanic tells me that the rotors need to be replaced. It's an expensive job but it has to be done. This will be the first of many unexpected expenses in the next year causing our savings account to shrink.

June 16

Today I am delighted to see that Russ's feeding tube is draped around the actual mechanism that delivers the only nourishment he has known since the cardiac arrest. The stomach tube remains intact since he will still be getting the oatmeal-colored feeding for part of the day. The nurse explains that they will slowly wean him off this feeding and replace it with actual food. What a wonderful milestone for him! Since he is not tethered to the feeding tube, I manage to maneuver the cumbersome chair out in the hallway. We go the entire length of both wings and into the dining room. I ask him if he'd like to go outside to which he replies "yes". It's a warm sunny day and I position the chair so he can feel its warmth. I lock the chair brakes so he doesn't slide off the slight incline. I ask him what he sees and he says "grass and trees". It feels so good to enjoy the outdoor freshness. Hopefully it will be an enriching experience for him. After a few minutes, he tells me that he has to go pee so I return him to his room, pull the curtains and get him a urinal. I empty the urinal, wash my hands and again instruct him how to use the call button when I am not here. *Does he understand? I have my doubts.*

June 17

    This is the last day of work before we enjoy a much-deserved 10-week summer break. It's a more relaxed day where many teachers show movies or play games during the half-day morning student schedule. The entire staff then goes out for a leisurely lunch after which we are free to leave. It allows us the rare chance to socialize and just relax. Even though I enjoy the time with my co-workers, my thoughts are as always with Russ. I will now be able to spend more time with him. He is my number one priority these days. Additionally, I only have to work one job, the one at the community college library. I work 16 hours a week during the summer, which allows me sufficient time to spend with Russ. I quickly exit the restaurant and bid my co-workers a good summer. Since Russ is again not attached to his feeding, I wheel him into the dining room where they are showing the movie "Homeward Bound". We watch the entire movie and then enjoy sitting outdoors for a while. When we return the nurse tells me that he is to be moved to the D Hall. He will be closer to the rehab unit. Russ greets her with a "hi, baby" and gives her a hug. This is so typical of the way he was, a charmer. Harlow and Dottie visit. Dottie asks Russ if he knows who Harlow is, but he still doesn't know. Dottie tells him that he needs to come home so he can mow the grass. It's been a good day.

June 18

This morning I walk into Russ's room but he is not there. When I see an aide walking toward me, I ask where he is. She tells me that he is in the dining room. I go to the dining room and find him sitting alone at a table. A tray with scrambled eggs, sausage and fruit juice is on the table. It doesn't look like he's eaten anything. I cut the sausage for him and hand him the fork. He then picks it up and starts to eat. There are a few aides present but they are helping distribute trays to the residents or feeding other residents who are unable to feed themselves. Would someone have gotten to Russ? I don't know but now I will arrive a little earlier so I can make sure he eats. At lunch I wheel him into the dining room where I assist him with the ravioli, milk, crushed pineapple and cottage cheese. They have also included a breadstick that I tear into small pieces to prevent choking. He eagerly eats the entire lunch, which must taste like a banquet after his tube feeding. After dinner I leave to go to a BBQ that I have been invited to. The invitation came from Stephanie's high school friend. I will welcome the rare chance to socialize. It's a welcome break from all the stress of hospitals, doctors and nursing homes that have become my norm.

June 19

I arrive just as breakfast is being served. Russ is already there, sitting alone again. He does well eating the egg, toast, hot cereal and grape juice. He carefully uses the fork and spoon to get every last bite. When we get back to the room, I notice that his glasses are not there. I look in his nightstand and windowsill without luck. The nurse comes in and I ask her about it. She says that they may have gotten misplaced when he got moved. This doesn't surprise me since they have misplaced some of his clothing too. I had to search their laundry area to find them. The nurse tells me that Russ only gets the tube feeding from 7pm to 7am. All his medication is administered by mouth. I leave the nursing home at 7:30pm so I can mow the lawn but when I attempt to start the lawn tractor, it won't turn over. I check the oil and gas. They are at acceptable levels. Tomorrow I'll ask a neighbor to look at it. This is the first of various household items that all of a sudden need repair. *This is not what I need now!*

June 20

Russ's breakfast consists of a scrambled egg, toast, oatmeal and cranberry juice. I keep him company while he eats without my assistance. Later in the morning his sister comes to visit him. Since he is in physical therapy, this gives her the opportunity to watch him as he goes through the exercises. He is now in the anti-gravity treadmill, a machine that consists of a pressure controlled chamber that gently lifts the patient but still allows for supportive walking. The therapist first puts the specialized shorts on Russ. These shorts have a zipper that is attached to the part of the machine that lifts him up. Russ walks on the machine for 15 minutes. It appears like he is barely floating above the treadmill floor. It's definitely a cool apparatus that looks like something the astronauts would practice on before a moonwalk. Once Russ is in the chair, the therapist hands him some weights and has him do some arm curls and lifts. He instructs Russ to push with his legs as the therapist resists the pushing. After lunch and all the physical therapy, Russ quickly falls asleep. I leave after his dinner but get a call at 10:00pm that he fell out of his chair and landed on his knees. They will take an X-ray of his knees to make sure nothing is broken. I head back to the nursing home. To my relief, the X-rays are negative. By midnight, Russ is in bed with the long cushion, protecting him from falling out of bed. I push the empty mattress next to his bed, just as an added precaution.

June 21

When I walk in the room this morning I notice a breakfast tray on bedside table. There are empty bowls, plates and a glass, evidence of a well-eaten breakfast. The bedside table is in front of him. He can definitely eat on his own if someone places the table within reach. Later in the morning I take Russ outside for a while. It is a warm, humid day but it feels good to be in the fresh air. He has been devoid of any outdoor breeze and this is a welcome contrast to the stale air in the nursing home. The physical therapist takes him down to the therapy room after lunch. Again Russ works out on the anti-gravity treadmill where he walks for 15 minutes. Afterwards, he is in front of the cycling machine, pedaling away for 10 minutes. He tires and wants to stop but the therapist encourages him to keep on working his leg muscles. The visiting doctor stops in Russ's room later to order a chest X-ray. This has been ordered because a nurse noticed that he's been coughing more than usual. The doctor says that pneumonia can be a problem in these facilities.

June 22

    Shortly after breakfast, Russ has a visit from the physical therapist. We all go to the physical therapy department where the therapist puts a gait belt on Russ. It is a cloth belt that is used to steady a patient. They have been using it when they have Russ walk across the therapy room. The therapist holds onto it as Russ walks. Today she shows me how to secure the belt and use it to transfer Russ from the chair to the toilet. I will need to do this when he is at home. Bill visits later in the morning. He comments that he likes the oldies station that we have on. He has been a good, loyal friend through all this. I get a call on my cell phone from the golf cart repair shop. They have replaced the batteries with new ones and can drop the cart off tomorrow. Although the batteries were very expensive, I felt the cost was justified since Russ always liked riding in the golf cart and we can use it this summer if he feels up to it. The speech therapist comes in around 2pm to work with Russ. She asks him how two items are alike such as beans and peas. He gets many of these items correct. She then quizzes him about different scenarios. For example, what would you do if you saw your neighbor's house on fire? He answers that he would call the fire department. She tells me that last week he got 1 out of 10 questions correct, but this week he answered 7 out of 10 correctly. This news is just what I needed to hear. He is making progress! Before I leave, the doctor comes in to remove his stomach tube. He explains that the opening will heal slowly from the inside. Another victory! It's been a hopeful day and I leave happy.

June 23

This morning's breakfast consists of a quiche, toast and hot cereal. Russ eats everything except for the cereal. He only eats some of it. Most of the morning consists of Russ resting or again singing along to some song from the 1950's that he hears on satellite radio. I need to find services for Russ when he comes home so I contact an organization in town that lends out medical equipment such as shower chairs and commode support bars. They are very helpful on the phone so I will make the trip there later in the week to borrow these items. We are fortunate that we have a walk-in shower and a hand-held showerhead. It will make giving Russ a shower that much easier. I also contact a place that acts as a resource center for seniors. The person I need to talk to is not in so I leave a message on his voicemail. I am looking for some assistance when Russ comes home and I have to go to work for 4 hours in the afternoon. Someone will have to stay with him while I'm at work. He won't be able to be left alone and I can't afford to pay someone on a continual basis. Maybe the agency can help me. Later, at work a person from the agency calls me back and says that they cannot help me. He suggests that I talk to the nursing home social worker. She has rarely been available and my initial encounter with her concerning Russ signing papers left me doubting her competency. That's all it takes. I burst into tears in our back room where I've taken the call. My supervisor Jill notices this and comforts me. I continue crying, saying that I can't get any answers. She can sense that this crying episode might last a while so she says that she will take my shift so I can go home. She does this after working an 8 -hour day prior to my arrival. Usually I work the 4- hour night shift alone. She even offers me some money so I can go out to dinner. I refuse this generous offer. Jill is and has always been the best boss and friend to me. She asks if I'll be ok to drive home. I do manage to drive but sob all the way. Instead of going home I find myself going to a nearby mall parking lot. I find an area with few cars and continue crying. I guess the enormity of the past few months has hit me all at once.

Stephanie calls me while I am in the midst of all this crying. As always, she manages to calm me down. She reminds me how wonderful I've been during all this, how strong and dedicated to Russ I've been. I don't know how I would have gotten through all this without her support. Her daily calls gave me the courage to get through the difficult days. She is the best daughter a mother could want. I am truly blessed to have her in my life! I am now calm and decide to stop to get a freshly made pizza to enjoy at home.

June 24

   Russ is eating an omelet in the dining room when I arrive. He seems disinterested in the cold cereal. He is gaining more control in eating with a fork or spoon. I leave the nursing home at 10:00am for a doctor's appointment. I have developed a rash that the doctor looks over and prescribes a cream for. When I return to the nursing home, Russ is in physical therapy where he is exercising on the cycling machine. He also does some unassisted walking across the room. I leave after supper to do grocery shopping followed by watching television. I fall asleep doing this.

June 25

Russ is lying in the bed when I arrive at the nursing home. I notice that his brief is wet, so I find a clean, dry one and proceed to help him change into it. It's been my experience here that to wait for a staff member to help a resident is a waste of time. The few staff members are busy tending to other residents. The lucky residents have family who assist them. I transfer Russ to the chair and secure him there while I position the bed tray containing his breakfast in front of him. He starts to eat the pancakes, sausage and hot cereal. Later, when the sun warms the air, I take Russ out for a while. But after a few minutes, he rubs his arms and says he's cold. We then go down the hall to see the resident who frequently peeks in Russ's room to say hello. She seems happy to see us and opens a box to reveal a powder blue nightgown that her sister bought her. I comment how pretty the nightgown is. She also points out an 8 x 10 portrait of her parents that she has placed on the windowsill. She says that she misses them even after all these years. It's getting close to suppertime so Russ and I make our way to the dining room. There we see a familiar older couple. The man usually arrives when I do to spend the day with his wife. I recognize his shorts and dark socks, his usual attire. He is with her all day just like I am with Russ. Although thin and somewhat frail-looking himself, he pushes her in the wheelchair down the halls or outside where they sit together. She is indeed a lucky woman to have such a devoted husband. I have observed that the other residents rarely have visitors except on Sundays when well-dressed family members come to visit.

June 26

This morning I once more find Russ in bed far from the bedside table that has his breakfast tray. If I didn't get here early enough, it would remain there until a staff member removed it. He would not get to eat any breakfast. *How do they expect him to get up to reach his breakfast?* I find an aide out in the hall to point out this situation. She does not reply but does help me get him into a chair and places the bedside table in front of him. He eagerly eats all the breakfast. Since it is cool this morning, we watch television for a while. I take him into the dining room for lunch. It's good for him to be in the company of others. By early afternoon, the sun has warmed the air and I take the opportunity to take Russ outside. The sun feels good on my skin and the gentle breeze is soothing. I leave to run an errand, returning just in time for supper. The tray is in his room. It consists of a tuna sandwich, chicken soup and strawberry shortcake for dessert. I'm glad that he hasn't eaten yet because he is allergic to strawberries. I remember telling the staff this and yet, there is the strawberry shortcake. I take it to the nurse and tell her that he cannot have strawberries. She apologizes for the mistake and will make sure the dietary department notes the allergy. This is the last thing he would need, an allergic reaction! It's another example of the incompetence in this facility.

June 27

Russ is in his chair this morning while his breakfast tray sits on the bedside table far out of his reach. An aide walks briskly in and tells me that he didn't want any breakfast. Nonsense! If someone would make the effort to encourage him to eat, it will certainly happen. I pull the bedside table in front of him and gently suggest that he eat the egg, toast and hot cereal before they get cold. He eats all of the breakfast. As I clear the tray, I notice the strong smell of urine. That's when I discover his very wet briefs and shorts. I check the hallway for an aide but do not find anyone. I then press the call light and wait. Several minutes pass without any response so I take matters into my own hands. I find a dry brief along with clean shorts in the closet. I proceed to get the wet ones off of him and put the dry ones on. He complains about being cold, so I get a blanket from the bed to cover him up. In the early afternoon, the physical therapist comes in to do range of motion exercises with Russ. They are unable to use the physical therapy room since publicity photos are being taken there.

June 28

I help Russ by moving his tray in front of him so he can eat breakfast. An hour later, the physical therapist arrives and takes him to the physical therapy where he has Russ walk 20 minutes in the anti-gravity treadmill. When we return to the room, Russ's daughters are there and greet him. They have brought family photo albums. Next to each portrait is the name of the family member. They show him each picture and ask if he knows whom the person is. He does recognize some photos but is not sure about others. After lunch, Russ is once again taken to physical therapy where the therapist hands him a 2-foot long pole that is labeled 5 pounds. She instructs him to raise the pole without bending his arms. She wants him to do this 20 times but he only manages 6 times. He says he is tired. I leave to go to my part-time job while his daughters visit with him. I get a call shortly before the end of my shift saying that Russ managed to undo the chair's safety straps and fell but quickly got on his feet. Thank goodness he is not injured. I check for any bumps or bruises. There are none.

June 29

Russ is sound asleep when I step into the room. I try to raise his head in an effort to wake him, but he refuses. He tells me to leave him alone.   Therefore, he doesn't eat breakfast. The speech therapist comes in shortly afterwards to do cognitive exercises. He is so drowsy that he only gets a few questions correct. This fatigue is persistent throughout the day. When I attempt to wake him so he can have lunch, he again tells me to leave him alone. Another missed meal. He doesn't even respond to the physical therapist who has come to work with him. The therapist can tell Russ is too tired so he says he will postpone the therapy until tomorrow. I haven't seen him so fatigued. I will mention it to the doctor although I suspect that it's indicative of the brain injury.

June 30

Russ is lying in bed this morning but his eyes are open and he appears to be more alert than yesterday. I use the power lever on the bed to raise his head. When it is high enough, I assist him in sitting up and swing his legs over the bedside. He is wet, along with his sheet and T-shirt. I manage to get a clean brief, shorts and T-shirt on him. He is easily transferred to the chair where he eats his breakfast. 30 minutes later, he announces that he has to go to the bathroom so I push the chair into the bathroom close to the toilet and help him sit on it. He uses the support bars on the toilet to steady himself. After a few minutes, he says he is done and I get him back into the chair. After lunch, the physical therapist comes in to take him to the therapy room. He releases the safety straps from the chair and has Russ walk the entire length of the room. Russ speeds up his pace and the therapist reminds him to slow down. He is walking very well. What a difference from yesterday's lethargic man. I take a break in the late afternoon to reluctantly talk to the social worker. Even though she is not one of my favorite people, I do need her help in getting a list of insurance approved home health agencies. I stop by her office and she hands me a list of local agencies.

July 1

I arrive to find Russ awake and alert in his chair. The tray in front of him has just a few morsels of uneaten food and it's obvious that he has eaten most of his breakfast. I go to the closet where I find some shorts, a T-shirt and a clean brief. I help him change into the clean clothes. The speech therapist comes into the room to quiz him on the date, month, year and season. He is still unaware of these events. She then asks him how apples, pears and peaches are alike. He answers that they are all types of fruit. More analogies are given and Russ is able to see the similarities in most examples. Soon after the speech therapist leaves, the physical therapist comes in to do exercises in the therapy room. Russ walks across the large therapy room with minimal assistance. He is then instructed to work out on the cycling machine. He does 20 minutes with a little encouragement from the therapist. I am very proud of him! We return to the room just in time for lunch. Since his tray is not in the room, we go to the dining room. The aide places a tray in front of Russ containing minced fish, corn, and noodles. He surprises me by eating the fish. Normally he does not care for fish, even though I'd like him to eat some. I do not mention that what he has just eaten is fish. Perhaps I can get him to eat fish at home if I also mince it and don't mention what it is. I'll give it a try. After lunch Russ finds the family photo album that his daughter left. He turns each page and as he does, I ask him if he knows the person's name. He only gets a few names correct. We will try doing this every day to see if more family members become familiar faces. The album is secured with two ribbons. To my amazement, he takes the two loose ribbon ends and ties them into a bow. I wouldn't have thought that he remembered how to tie a bow. Before I depart, I ask him if he has to use the bathroom. He says that he does, so I walk him to the bathroom and have him wash his hands afterwards. I leave, pleased with his progress. He has come so far from those days when he was unresponsive, attached to every variety of medical devices.

July 2

Russ is in bed today in a deep sleep. He is so tired that he skips breakfast and lunch. It's one of those days when he is more interested in sleeping than eating. This is a pattern that will continue throughout his recovery. I attribute it to the brain injury and realize that his brain requires the rest. Since he is so tired today, I go home to mow the lawn and do a few chores. When I return at 5:30 I find Russ awake, sitting in the chair. Since I notice that his shorts are wet, I put clean shorts on him. Dinner is now being served in the dining room. He must be ravenous after skipping breakfast and lunch. The dinner consists of pork roast, au gratin potatoes, bread and pudding. I help him cut the pork into small, manageable pieces. He eagerly eats all his dinner but says that I should have something to eat too. He offers me some of his dinner but I decline, saying that I have already eaten mine at home. This gesture is so typical of him. He is the type of person who is always willing to help others. Before his illness, he would have a Thanksgiving dinner for those who had no one to share this special day with. He paid for the entire dinner without asking for any donations. We usually had 20-30 people in the clubhouse for this Thanksgiving dinner. It was a lot of work but I know he received so much satisfaction from doing this.

July 3

Today is another tired day for Russ. He manages to eat breakfast, though, but falls asleep soon after it. This fatigue causes him to miss lunch. I sit with him and occupy my time writing in my journal, reading the latest issue of the AARP newsletter and doing research on brain injury. He does awake in time to eat all of his supper but soon falls asleep again.

July 4

Russ is in the chair eating his breakfast when I get to the nursing home. I'm glad to see that the staff has positioned the tray so he can easily access it. After breakfast I change his clothes. As I finish, the physical therapist comes in to take Russ to the therapy room. Just as he starts to walk, a friend of ours, Jon arrives to watch Russ do his therapy. He tells him that he wants to see him walk. Russ replies that he'll "think about it". Jon then calls his wife, Helen, so she can persuade Russ to walk. He hands the phone to Russ. I can't hear what Helen is saying, but Russ nods and tells her "ok" several times. She must have said something very convincing because Russ walks the entire length of the large room several times. Afterwards, Jon and I take Russ outside. Jon says he will pick Helen up in order to join us. In a few minutes, Jon and Helen pull into a nearby parking spot. They pull up chairs next to us and we all enjoy the warm, sunny day. An hour passes when Jon announces that they must leave since Helen's sister from Chicago will be arriving soon to spend the week with them. I thank them for their visit and concern.

July 5

Today I make it my mission to talk to the doctor so when I see the nurse near the medication cart in the hall, I tell her that I'd like to see him when he comes in. She agrees to this. At 9:30 an aide takes Russ to give him a shower. I ask her if I can accompany him. I would like to see how they transfer him from the chair to the shower since I will soon have to do this task at home. They have him walk from the chair to a bench in the shower where they have him use a washcloth to cleanse himself. He is rinsed with a hand-held showerhead, similar to what we have at the house. I'm glad we installed one several years ago. I leave for lunch at 11:30 and when I return I ask the nurse when the doctor will arrive for visits. She tells me that he has already made his rounds. Just my luck, the one hour I'm gone, that's when he is at the nursing home. She adds that the doctor will be back tomorrow. Later in physical therapy Russ walks the entire length of the room again with minimal assistance. The therapist holds Russ's gait belt as he walks. It's amazing to see him walk so well.

July 6

This morning I move Russ's breakfast tray so he can actually reach it. The staff has again left it on the other side of the room, far beyond his ability to get it. I am determined today to talk with the nursing home doctor. There are several questions I'd like to ask him. All morning, I glance out into the hall toward the nursing station. The doctor will surely begin his duties by reviewing the residents' charts. Finally at 11:00am, I see him at the station reading a chart. I seize the opportunity to talk to him. I begin with an "excuse me, I am Russ's wife and I'd like to ask you a few questions". Without looking up from the chart, he

states that the physician's assistant will help me. I
see a younger man, probably in his late 30's,
examining a chart. I ask if he is the physician's
assistant and he answers affirmatively. I tell him
Russ's name and add that I need some questions
answered. He takes Russ's chart and leads me into
the lobby, away from curious ears. I rattle off the
questions- when can he wean Russ off the sedatives?
, What kind of care will Russ need once he is home? ,
What kind of prognosis can he give me? , When will
he write the discharge papers? He listens intently to
all my questions and answers them honestly. The
one thing I've learned throughout this experience is
how vague the doctors are about Russ's condition
and prognosis. Since day 1, I've heard the same
words.... time will tell, each brain injury is different. I
suppose they don't want to give families false hope so
it's easier to be evasive. Stephanie sent me a
necklace with a square locket. Upon the locket was
the simple word, hope. Even when Russ was in
coma, dodging death, I only had hope. Whenever I
feel depressed, I feel the necklace and cling to that
word, hope. It gives me the courage to endure the
difficult days.

July 7
    Today my morning consists of spending time with
Russ, who is especially tired today. Just being with
him though, makes me happy. He awakes in time for
lunch but takes another nap shortly after eating. I
take this opportunity to check into resources that may
be available to him and me. This is all new to me and
it is frustrating because I am unfamiliar with where to
go for help. Most of what I have learned, I stumbled
upon by searching the Internet. I realize that
someone will have to supervise Russ when I am at

work. My summer hours are 16 hours per week so hopefully I can find people to be with him. I drive to the county building where an agency for seniors is located. I find the office but the woman at the desk is on a call. I sit and wait until she is finished. Then I explain our situation. I really need what is called "custodial care". It is necessary to our budget that I work, but Russ cannot be left alone. Someone will have to be with him. She explains that my only option is to hire someone to help out or have friends or family stay with him. I really don't have the money to hire someone so I will swallow my pride and ask friends. I leave disappointed that there is no help in such situations. I will manage somehow, though.

July 8

This morning I arrive to find Russ awake eating his breakfast of Cheerios, an egg and some toast. I'm grateful that for once, his bedside table with the tray has been placed in front of him so he can reach his food. Shortly after breakfast, Russ falls asleep. I step outside to call the case manager at the insurance company. We discuss the discharge plans for Russ. She says that a nurse, physical therapist and occupational therapist will visit him at home. I ask if there is any way that the insurance company will pay for someone to watch him while I work. She replies that this is "custodial" care and is not a benefit. I don't like to ask for help but I must now, for Russ's sake.

July 9

    The nursing home doctor comes into the room by early morning to say that next Wednesday will be Russ's discharge date. He quickly leaves after making the announcement. An hour later the social worker steps in to hand me a list of home health agencies. I am to choose one and let her know. She will then make the arrangements. None of the agencies are in our hometown. The closest one is 20 miles away. I don't understand this since our town has at least 75,000 people and one would think there are at least several agencies close by. Perhaps the insurance company dictates the choice. I choose the closest agency. The social worker will arrange for a wheelchair. This is a covered benefit. He will need a shower bench and toilet rails. I have found an organization in town that lends these items to people. We will be able to keep them for a year.

July 10

Russ is napping when I arrive, leaving an uneaten breakfast on the tray. By 11am he finally awakes. I use the opportunity to encourage him to eat lunch in the dining room. He eagerly finishes the Salisbury steak, mashed potatoes but leaves the carrots. Although I wish he would eat more vegetables, I learned a long time ago that he only favors corn and peas. Arguing about it has proven a waste of time. Sometimes he is indeed stubborn. I suggest that we go to see his former roommate. I push the cumbersome chair to the room only to find it empty. There is a lounge at the end of the hall where some residents use to watch television or enjoy the overstuffed sofas. We find his roommate there engrossed in a baseball game on TV. I greet him with a hello. He turns around and smiles at us. I maneuver Russ's chair so we can face him and talk. The roommate tells us that he used to work near Milwaukee Avenue in Chicago. It is the Polish area of the city where many immigrants settled. He remembers that the women used to make small dumplings filled with potato, sauerkraut or plums. According to him, he really enjoyed the delicious flavors that the ladies would give him. I tell him that these are called pierogis. My mother would make wonderful pierogis for us. When I return home I call several of our good friends and Russ's customers to get help in watching him while I work. If I can get each person to commit to a 4-hour slot one day a week, I would really make my life easier. As I call each person, I ask for help in doing this and mention that this would be on a non-paid basis. I don't have the money to pay for the entire time involved. I do mention that I could get them small gifts instead. Every person I call turns me down with a variety of excuses. Some said they didn't have the time, are afraid of liability, couldn't do it but gave no reason why or simply say "no". Even our good friends Connie and Rick who joined us many times for breakfast at a local restaurant and went to Arizona with us turned me down. Jon and Helen also refuse to help. People have disappointed me during points in my life but this rejection really hurts me deeply. These people were supposed to be friends, somebody you could count on during the hard times. Yet they turned their back on Russ and me. Russ, who always helped them on some project or let them borrow a tool, now was forgotten. I had to swallow my pride by then asking some neighbors. This was extremely difficult for me to do since I don't like asking for help. But I reminded myself that it was for Russ, not for me. Several of my neighbors turned out to be the most help by volunteering to watch Russ. Most of them were people I only said hello to previously. Ed, Roxanne, Jodi, Bill and Judy helped out. I will always be grateful to them for their generosity. Another neighbor, Arlene, was especially helpful and would later become a paid caregiver.

July 11

I use the morning to visit Russ who is more awake today. The afternoon is devoted to picking up the items I will need for him at home. I am very grateful for the organization that will let us borrow the needed medical equipment. I pick up toilet support rails, a bed rail and a shower chair. Just a mile from this lending organization is a medical supply store. I buy a gait belt there since I know I will need one to support Russ when he walks. Although he is stronger, he nevertheless remains quite weak. The gait belt will assist me in getting him around at home. When I return to the nursing home in time for his dinner, he is in the chair with wet shorts and top. I again change these for him. Who knows how long he's been like this. I will be so glad when he's out of this place!

July 12

I wake up with the anticipation that Russ only has one day left at the nursing home. Although this was a necessary transition before returning home, it has hardly been ideal. The nurses administer his medication and the aides take his vital signs but most of the time he is left on his own. I've tried to provide some stimulus by playing the radio, taking him outside and keeping him company for much of the day. This afternoon I have him stretch his legs. He is not receiving any more physical therapy so I must take over in order for his legs to remain limber. I am surprised to see the occupational therapist come in to again ask him if he knows what day, month and season it is. He fails to answer these correctly. He does, however, do better when asked to tell the similarities and differences between objects.

July 13

I am so excited to have Russ come home today! The last time he was at the house was that terrible night of April 11. So much has happened since then. Somehow he has managed to survive an almost fatal condition. I hope I will be able to give him the best care possible. Even though I am not a medical professional, I will try to do so. I ask myself, can a 5'0 woman like myself care for a 6'0" man? The one thing I have going for me is that for someone my size, I am physically strong. The past few months have shown that I am mentally strong too. I will need both these assets to care for Russ. The doctor comes in to check Russ's heart and lungs. Soon afterwards, the nurse arrives with discharge papers for me to sign. Our friend, Bill P. comes to help. I asked him to bring his mid-sized car so Russ could easily get into it. The step into our SUV is too high for someone in his fragile condition. We are just waiting on the wheelchair to arrive. The other day the social worker ordered one for us. After 20 minutes, Bill goes to the nursing station to check on this. He returns to report that the nurse says a wheelchair will be delivered to the house. We need one now, though, to use at home. I talk to her and she agrees to let us borrow one of their wheelchairs. I quickly gather his clothes from the closet and remove the flowers from the windowsill. Bill pushes the wheelchair down the hall and outside. Finally we are out of this dreary place! When we arrive home, Bill and I help Russ walk into the house. I have Russ sit in the recliner where I cover him with a blue throw. He is so sensitive now to cold and heat. He is soon settled in the chair and soon falls asleep. I ask Bill if he can stay with Russ so I can fill his prescriptions. I did not want to stop at the pharmacy before but was anxious to get Russ home.

I pick up the prescriptions and some disposable briefs before heading home. Russ is still taking 2 mood stabilizers. He is being weaned off the 1 stabilizer and should soon be off of it completely. I will talk to his family doctor about the other one. I thank Bill for his help and after he leaves, I organize all Russ's medications into a daily medication container. He already had this before he got sick. The ironic thing is that he was previously on daily cholesterol medication I also make a chart of what medication he takes in the morning and at night. The fact that he takes 8 different pills a day necessitates this. I make us a dinner of roast pork, mashed potatoes and corn. I put the wheelchair alongside the recliner and move the now awake Russ to the wheelchair. I have removed the regular dining room chair from the table to make room for the wheelchair. He clumsily holds the fork but does manage to use it to eat the entire contents of his plate. I have cut the meat for him since his fine motor skills are not adequate yet. By 9:30pm he is again falling asleep so I place him into the wheelchair and bring him into the bedroom. He is finally in his own bed after all these months. He sleeps peacefully until 8am.

July 14

When Russ awakes, I get him into the wheelchair and take him to the bathroom. He uses the toilet after which I wash and dry him. I apply protective cream to his anal area. I was instructed to do this by the nurses in order to prevent sores. Russ puts on the clean T-shirt and shorts that I have placed near him. I instruct him to comb his hair and brush his teeth. He then eats the breakfast of an omelet, sausage and toast that I made for him. After I return him to the recliner, the phone rings. It is the visiting nurse who states that she is on her way to see him. When she arrives, we go through his medication list. She also takes his blood pressure and temperature. Shortly after the nurse departs, Roxanne, our neighbor, comes in to watch Russ, She will stay with him from 3:30pm-8: 30pm while I work. Even though I feel guilty about leaving him, I do have to work in order to pay the bills. Russ continues to get Social Security but we need my income to support us.

July 15

Russ goes through his usual morning routine of going to the bathroom, brushing his teeth and combing his hair. Because he is still weak, I use the wheelchair to move him around in the house. Today when I apply the protective cream, I notice that his skin is not as red as before. I'm sure that my keeping his skin dry and clean has helped. I suspect that he would sit for a long time in a wet brief in the nursing home before anyone changed him. That certainly kept his skin irritated. I need to go to the grocery store so I call my boss and friend Jill to see if she can stay with him. She kindly agrees to this. I have often said that she is the best boss I've ever had and this action proves it. Russ is tired this evening so we go to bed around 9pm.

July 16
    We settle into our morning routine of waking up, cleaning up in the bathroom, dressing and breakfast. I am happy that I have summers off from school especially now so I can care more for Russ. So far, the transition to the house has been good. He hasn't said so but I'm sure he is more comfortable in his own home. The physical therapist calls to say she will be here between 4-5pm. I take him into the spare bedroom where the computer is. I want to find a computer game he can play to strengthen his mental skills. We search a game called "Bursting Balloons". The object of the game is to burst all the same color balloons that are next to each other. Russ was able to match the color balloons, although he did this more slowly than I did. But maybe if we do this from time to time, his reflexes will improve. We only spend a few minutes on this since I don't want to tire him too much. At 5:30pm the physical therapist calls to get directions, saying she is lost downtown. I give her exact directions to the house. When she arrives, she

has Russ raise and lower his legs. She also has him stand by the kitchen sink where she instructs him to stand on his toes, raise his leg to the side and bend his legs. He is able to do this easily.

July 17

I awake at 7am to find that Russ is already awake. I ask him if he'd like to get out of bed. He says "ok" to that. After our morning routine, he falls asleep again. Kip calls in the afternoon but Russ is asleep. She asks how he is doing and is pleased to hear that things are good. Kip was born near here like all Russ's siblings but moved to the West coast when she was a teenager. Russ comes from a large family, some of who moved out of state, but some have remained nearby. When he awakes, I dial Kip's number and have him talk to her. She is thrilled to hear his voice. After dinner, I suggest that he should take a shower. I push him into the bathroom, remove his clothes and have him sit on the shower bench that I placed in the shower. I put shower gel on a washcloth to have him lather himself. We installed a hand-held showerhead several years ago and now it has definitely made this task easier. I am easily able to rinse him off and wash his hair. He reaches for the grab bar to get out of the shower. I quickly dry him and get his pajamas on before putting him to bed.

July 18-31

During this time period, we fall into a regular routine. A semblance of normalcy has returned. For the first time in a long time, we are together. Even though his fatigue makes him sleep for a good portion of the day, I cherish his presence. We enjoy meals at the same table or watch television in each other's company. The nurse, physical and occupational therapist visit throughout this period. On one of her visits the nurse brings a social worker along. She inquires how Russ and I are doing. She is concerned since she says that being a caregiver is very stressful. Am I getting enough help? I tearfully explain that I am getting very little help; even from people I thought I could count on. I have always cried when I am stressed. Maybe it's a bad thing but I suppose it's my coping mechanism. I cry, get it out and then I am better. I've been crying continuously since April. The social worker tells me about a state program that will pay for some of Russ's supplies and respite time for me. Since he became ill, I have had very little time for myself. She will help me apply for this program. I didn't know it then but this program would prove to be invaluable. Then as our life seemed to be settling down, Russ falls one day and breaks his finger. I felt so guilty. In spite of watching him carefully, I left him unattended and he hurt himself. He is taken to the hospital emergency room where they set his finger and keep him for a few days because he also hit his head. They give him a powerful antibiotic since his hand is somewhat red. They are concerned about an infection. He is released with instructions to see the orthopedist in one week.

August 2011

My neighbors have been kind enough to watch Russ while I work. I have set up a schedule of having each person take I day of my 4-day workweek. Bill P. has even taken a day although he is becoming short of breath and needs a portable oxygen machine to help him breathe. He has gone to a specialized hospital on the east side of our state to determine what is causing his breathing difficulties. They will schedule a lung biopsy soon in order to determine whether any abnormalities exist. I give my neighbors small treats from the dollar store for their help. It's not much but it's all I can afford and I want to show my deep appreciation for their kindness.

One night in early August, I am awakened in the middle of the night by a nauseous smell. It is a combination of feces and rotting flesh or something close to that. *Did the dog have an accident?* I turn my bedside lamp on. The dog is sleeping next to the dresser. I look around and go to Russ's side of the bed and am horrified to see him, his pajamas and parts of the bed linens covered in a dull yellowish-brown liquid. It's obviously diarrhea but not the kind I've ever seen. I quickly grab some disposable vinyl gloves from the adjacent bathroom, a plastic bag and a clean brief. I transfer the soiled pad, pajamas and bed linens to the washing machine, throwing them in. I clean Russ with a wet washcloth until all traces of the diarrhea are eradicated. Before Russ was released from the nursing home, I purchased some clear plastic to put between the mattress pad and the mattress. He would be incontinent and I didn't want our recently new mattress ruined. This night the plastic would protect the mattress. After all this drama, I turn over to get some sleep. But he would have repeated bouts of this diarrhea all night long. He goes through many briefs and still it keeps coming. Finally at 5am I manage to get him into the car. This is far from normal. He seemed to be getting weak but did his best to walk to the car. It was time to go to the emergency room.

We spend the next 7 hours in the emergency room where they did blood tests and fecal tests. Russ is dehydrated so they replace his fluids with an IV solution. Only then did his face color come back. Before this, he had an almost ghost-white look to his face and dark circles around his eyes. The strange diarrhea kept coming, letting up for only short periods. Finally the doctor came in with a diagnosis: C-Diff. I had never heard of this. I asked how Russ could have gotten it. It can easily live on surfaces for a long time so he could have gotten it from the previous hospitalization or from antibiotic therapy. He has to be admitted to the hospital for a few days so they could get this under control. The hospital room can only be entered when one puts on a yellow disposable gown and washes their hands before leaving the room. It is Tuesday and after a treatment of IV's, and Vancomycin he is released on the following Saturday. He is given a prescription for more Vancomycin that I have to administer for 10 days.

I made it my mission to learn more about this evil thing called C-Diff. By searching the Internet, I found out that C-Diff is resistant and difficult to treat. Also, one way to contract it is by using antibiotics. Antibiotics kill bad bacteria but they can also destroy the good bacteria in the colon. We need the good bacteria for proper functioning of the colon. If the good bacteria are eliminated, harmful bacteria can take over. C-Diff is one such harmful bacterium. When Russ returned home, I had him sign a medical release form that I took to the hospital medical records department. I remembered the antibiotic given to him in July. Sure enough, there was the name of an antibiotic administered to him twice daily for 3 days. 600 mg were given to him at a time, for a total of 1200mg every 24 hrs. It seemed like a very high dosage to me. No wonder his good bacteria was eliminated. Later, the doctors would all tell me the same thing: any antibiotic could do this. But as I did my own research, I found out that certain antibiotics have an increased probability of causing C-Diff. The particular antibiotic that Russ had was at the top of the list of C-Diff causing antibiotics. I am angry with the medical professionals for using such a strong antibiotic when another safer one would suffice.

Once home, Russ looks much better. He has his appetite back plus the intense diarrhea is gone. I use this opportunity and time off from my part-time job (they had semester break) to search for a daytime caregiver. I would return to my full-time job in September. Someone had to look after Russ when I was at work. I make flyers to put in my neighbors' paper boxes, ran an ad in the newspaper and pinned some flyers in local grocery stores. I offer a small salary, less than minimum wage. Hopefully someone who needs a few extra dollars would reply. I interviewed a few nearby people but they either changed their minds or failed any background checks I ran. School was scheduled to start in 3 weeks; I had to secure a caregiver. My wonderful daughter Stephanie came through again. She put the word out on Facebook and a high school classmate responded that she would be happy to do it. I was overjoyed with the prospect of finally finding a good caregiver. Amanda, my new caregiver, does an admirable job between September and December. She is and will always be special to me. I am truly grateful for her work and dependability. What a load off my mind!

I decide to retire from my full-time job in December when I reach the age of 62 and can collect Social Security.

Everything is quiet at home as we once again settled into our routine. Then one week after I administered the last dose of Vancomycin, Russ has projectile vomiting at breakfast. The C-Diff diarrhea started again with a vengeance. It is almost too much for me to deal with the mess and misery of it. Once more, we were on our way to the emergency room. Blood tests and stool samples were run again. The C-Diff had returned. Russ spent 5 days in the hospital undergoing more Vancomycin treatment. The doctors added a probiotic in an effort to control the C-Diff. Upon his release, I am again given a prescription for Vancomycin, this time for 3 weeks. As I had done before, I wipe every surface down, especially in the bathrooms with a bleach solution. Although C-Diff is able to live on surfaces for a long time, bleach is one of the few items that will destroy it. Keeping everything disinfected with bleach helped since I never did get C-Diff.

September 2011
The school year has begun so I get ready to return to work. It will be good to see my co-workers and especially the kids. I've always enjoyed working with children. Their enthusiasm and energy keep me feeling young. This year, however, I am adjusting my routine. I will awake at 5am, get myself ready, make dinner to be eaten later in the day and get Russ's clothes ready. I feel guilty about getting him up at 6:20am. He should be sleeping later but I must get

him fed and have him take his medication. I am not paying Amanda enough to do this. It's a responsibility that I will take on. Besides, he can go back to sleep after breakfast when I have him sit in his recliner. Amanda arrives at 7:00 am and I take off for work. I then return to the house at 3:30pm and immediately take Russ to use the bathroom. Amanda leaves and a volunteer caregiver comes in at 3:45pm so I can get to my part-time job that starts at 4:00pm. Finally at 8:20pm I get home, we have dinner and are in bed at 9:15pm. On Saturdays I am required to work from 10am to 2pm. It is difficult to get volunteer caregivers on weekdays and impossible to get anyone on Saturdays. Therefore, I load Russ in the car along with his wheelchair and head off to work. We have a quiet workroom adjacent to the front desk. I put him there along with a packed lunch and videos for him to watch. It is not an ideal situation but I have to do it. Most of the time he would just sleep. We have very few people in on Saturdays and I doubt if anyone knew he was there. This would be my grueling daily schedule for the next 4 months. Looking back, I still don't know how I did it.

The next 25 days are uneventful until one Sunday in late September when after another round of Vancomycin is discontinued, the diarrhea returns. This time, though Russ complains of having to urinate frequently, little is expelled. We again find ourselves at the emergency room upon advice from his family doctor. A stool and urine sample is collected and to my surprise the stool sample is negative for C-Diff. It sure has the unique color and odor of C-Diff. The urine sample showed that he has a urinary tract infection. He is kept overnight and is released with a prescription to control the diarrhea plus another to treat the urinary tract infection.

I take September 30 off since I still have many vacation days that I haven't used. Besides, I need a "mental health" day. I take Russ to the ophthalmologist's office to get a new pair of glasses. He broke his old ones when he fell. The office hands me a medical history form to fill out. When Russ's name is called I remind the nurse that he is brain injured. He is given eye drops in order to dilate his eyes. Soon afterwards, he almost faints in the chair and his blood pressure drops. The ophthalmologist calls for an ambulance. He does not want to take any chances. Again, we find ourselves at the emergency room. Russ is kept overnight for observation.

October 2011

Russ's family doctor orders another refill of Vancomycin to keep the C-diff under control. He does very well while on the Vancomycin and shortly after it is discontinued the C-Diff returns. It has developed into this type of pattern. One night during the third week of October, I am awakened by the smell of the putrid diarrhea and tremors that consume Russ's upper body. They are so pronounced that they shake the entire bed. After cleaning him up, the tremors persist for another 2 hours. I tell myself this is not normal and it is frightening me. We make yet another trip to the emergency room. We arrive at 4am. This time, a diagnosis of C-Diff is made. He might have low potassium so he is given an IV with potassium. I am very frustrated with this persistent C-Diff and tell the doctor that we have to do something to finally eradicate it, once and for all. She senses my anger and then explains what I already know: that C-

Diff is resistant and it might take a while to control it. Russ is released in 6 days.

November 2011

This month comes and goes without any hospital admissions for Russ. After so many months of hospitals, doctors, emergency rooms, it feels great to be at relative peace at home. Although the diarrhea has diminished, the C-Diff stubbornly hangs on. It is controlled only by repeated doses of Vancomycin. I also give Russ probiotics in an attempt to restore his colon's beneficial bacteria. He has lost much weight during these difficult months. Hopefully he can regain this weight soon.

I use another vacation day to take Russ to the local Social Security office where I hope he will be approved for Social Security Disability Income. I push the wheelchair to an empty spot where it will be easy for the both of us to get up quickly. Russ almost falls asleep during this pause. We wait in a large room along with about 30 other people. Finally his name is called and I push the wheelchair to a more private area where an employee at a desk asks questions such as the name of his doctors, the dates of his hospitalizations and such. Russ is asked to sign some papers. He signs these slowly with much difficulty. I can hardly make out his name. The interviewer seems satisfied with his signature. Contrary to what I've heard, Russ quickly gets approved in 7 weeks. It must have been obvious from the medical records that he is indeed permanently disabled and would not be able to work.

All services such as physical, occupational and speech therapy have been discontinued. Although I can understand that Russ is making sufficient progress in occupational and speech therapy, I don't understand why he is no longer getting physical therapy. It was so beneficial in the nursing home and here at home. But apparently insurance companies have their rules so he will not be receiving any more physical therapy. I took mental notes of the exercises the physical therapist had him do at home. I will continue to do these with him on a daily basis. Thanksgiving is almost here and with it 4 days without work. I am very grateful since these 60 hr work-weeks are taking a toll on me. I've always had stamina but these few months have left me exhausted. My only hope is that retirement is just a month away. Our Thanksgiving is quiet with only the two of us. After Thanksgiving, I receive the wonderful news that Russ has been approved for the Area Agency on Aging program that the nursing service's social worker helped me apply for in July. He had been on a waiting list since then. Finally they have an opening. The program would now pay Amanda. Russ would also get a monthly supply of briefs and Boost nutritional drink. After I retire in January, the program plans to provide a caregiver so I can have some respite time. The purpose of the program is to have older people remain in their own home instead of a nursing home. I feel as if a tremendous load has been lifted off my shoulders.

December 2011

In only 3 weeks, I will be retiring. Earlier in the fall, I wrote my letter of intent to retire and sent 1 letter to the principal, another to the superintendent and another to Human Resources. In addition, I applied for my state's public school employee pension and Social Security. I have mixed feelings about retiring. I know that Russ needs me as caregiver but I will truly miss working with our students. Even during the most challenging times with them, they have left me with great memories. Our staff usually goes to a local bowling alley/restaurant on the last day before the 2- week holiday break. We get a rare chance to socialize, participate in a secret Santa and a White Elephant event. This year I am 1 of 2 people who are retiring. The principal graciously acknowledges my achievements and presents me with a gift certificate from the staff. I am also handed a gift certificate from the reading teacher. She and I have worked collaboratively. I will miss this amazing woman who always puts the students first. Staff members start to trickle out of the gathering. I say my final goodbyes while everyone wishes me the best. This is it. I made it through almost 4 months of 16-hour days. People near me do not know how I survived such a grueling schedule. I remind them that I had to do it. It's amazing what you can accomplish if you put your mind to it. I had to provide for Russ and me so I did whatever it took. However, I am very grateful that I am finished with it. Russ and I spend Christmas with my sister in a neighboring state. It is so good to see her, Charlie and their children again. Stephanie, Neil and baby Karina have also arrived. Russ is still so fatigued and naps most of the visit in their living room chair.

Shortly after Christmas, Bill's friend calls to tell me that he has died. I can hardly believe her words. The last thing I knew, he was in the university hospital 2 hours away scheduled for a lung biopsy. He died of respiratory failure. I am very upset to learn about this. He was such a good, loyal friend to us. I will always remember the good times we shared with him: enjoying the Polish festival at St. Stan's, going out to a favorite restaurant or simply dropping by his house where we would all talk and laugh. Russ especially took much pleasure in teasing Jenny, Bill's daughter.

January 2012

Today is the first unscheduled day of my retirement. I awake at 7:30am to enjoy some time alone in the living room, content to sip on morning coffee. I will not work at all during January because of a stipulation that forbids me from working I month after my official retirement date. It has to do with the state pension system. After the previous 4 months, I really need the rest. I am finally able to relax a bit. During the second week of January I attend a memorial for Bill. Roxanne is kind enough to watch Russ for me. Bill has been cremated, according to his wishes. The memorial at the church is indeed beautiful. The priest talked about how Bill always put his religion into practice. He was not one who just went to church on Sunday and then failed to honor his church's teachings during the week. He lived his faith 7 days a week. Russ does not remember Bill. I am grateful for this since he would be heartbroken for the loss of his best friend.

February 2012

This month I return to work at the library. Although the past month has at last been somewhat relaxing, I am glad to be back at work. Since I still do not have respite time, my work will give me a break from the responsibilities of being a caregiver. Ed, a neighbor, has agreed to be Russ's caregiver while I'm at work. The waiver program will pay for his services. It's a relief for me to finally have 1 consistent caregiver for Russ. Russ knows Ed and they get along well. I will be eternally thankful for the kindness of those neighbors who stepped up to help us.

Although the C-Diff has stubbornly hung on, the episodes of diarrhea are less severe. I cringe though when Russ complains of abdominal pain. It usually means that diarrhea will come. I've gotten quite good at disinfecting everything he comes in contact with. It must be working since I have not been affected by the dreaded C-Diff. It amazes me how he endured the inflammation in his weakened state. But I think that his colon is finally responding to the medication. C-Diff is a terrible condition that I would not wish on my worst enemy.

March 2012

Russ's social worker comes to see how he is doing. He is having a good day and greets her with open arms. She seems pleased with his progress. I explain that he has his good days, like today when he is more alert and bad days, when he is more interested in sleeping than anything else. She asks if he has had any further hospitalizations or falls. She also asks how his temperament is and how I am doing. I am entitled to respite time and she encourages me to take this. I will have to find someone to watch Russ. Perhaps there is a person nearby who can use some extra money and would be willing to do it.

I continue to research brain injury and find a link to the Brain Injury Association. Their home Web page mentions support groups. I find a group that meets in our town every Thursday afternoon. I help Russ into the car on the next Thursday so we can check out the support group. Members of the group welcome us and each person tells about their brain injury. Some have been hit by a car, fell off ladders, had an aneurysm or a stroke. I immediately feel at home with these people. They are friendly and understand the scope of brain injury. Once a month the group has an activity. It could be a picnic, a trip to a restaurant, the zoo or a game of bingo and pizza. I have learned much because of the speakers that come to the meetings. It's been very therapeutic to Russ and me.

Stephanie continues to call daily. I know she is concerned about Russ and me. Her recent postings of Karina's photos bring me so much joy. Karina seems to be a happy baby. I attribute this to the excellent parenting of Stephanie and Neil. They truly love their daughter. When Stephanie was a baby, I took her to the supermarket, on walks and to her grandma's house. I am glad that Stephanie is exposing Karina to the world around her. Since Stephanie's birthday is on the 28th, I have sent her a gift certificate to her favorite clothing store. Hopefully she will have some time to pick out something just for her. It's been a stressful time for her in many ways. I know she worries about us plus caring for a new baby.

April 2012

    I can hardly believe that it's been a year since Russ's cardiac arrest. The year has been tumultuous but the fact that he has survived so much adversity is amazing. Since the weather is getting warmer I have taken him on short walks outside. He uses a walker that has a seat. He walks for a while and then must sit for a short time. The constant fatigue remains a problem for him. What surprises me is that he can read. He likes to read the mail although he cannot read all the words or understand the content. His digestive system is almost back to normal. Although he still sees snakes in the bathroom or outside, these incidents are decreasing in frequency.

    Karina and Russ share the same birthday on April 18 so we take a flight out to Virginia to help celebrate Karina's first birthday and Russ's first survival year. I am anxious about how Russ will do during the flight. I take the wheelchair and check it at the gate. Russ then walks to our seats. I brought my iPod so he can listen to some oldies. This might help him to relax and enjoy the flight. Throughout the time on the plane, he acts as though this is an everyday occurrence. Before long, we are at Reagan National Airport where Stephanie picks us up. I am relieved at the ease of the flight with Russ. The next day is Karina's party. Stephanie has invited her friends and their children. Most of the children are Karina's age. It was great to see all the children having fun playing with toys and even going to a nearby park.

May 2012- May 2013

In May 2012 I find a neighbor, Arlene, who is willing to watch Russ while I have some respite time. The waiver program is to pay for her services. We agree on 12 hours per week. For the first time in over a year I have some time to myself. I use the time to walk a nature trail, grocery shop by myself, do gardening and/or yard work and write this book. Arlene proves to be invaluable. She is dependable, kind plus she fixes Russ lunch and washes the dishes. He seems to like her company and cooperates with her. She even brings some games such as Monopoly and cards so they can play these. I bought Connect Four, Bingo and Uno to add to the collection. Sometimes on Sundays, we play the games. He gets excited when he wins. The games are a fun way to exercise his brain.

There are free outdoor summer concerts in our town. I get a schedule of the concert dates so we can attend them. During the summer we go to almost every concert. All we need is Russ's wheelchair and a folding chair for me. I bring bottled water for him so he doesn't get dehydrated. He enjoys the concerts immensely, so much so that he sings along to familiar songs. The Beatles Tribute is one of his favorites. I think he sang along to almost every song. Even when he was in the nursing home, he responded so positively to music. The concerts are an easy way to get him out of the house and do something he truly enjoys.

One early summer morning, Russ astonishes me by walking out of the bedroom. He says "hi" and stops, unsure of what to do next. Since he only has his pajamas on, I go to him and suggest that he use the bathroom, after which I will get his clothes out. He slowly manages to put his jeans, t-shirt, underwear and socks on. The fact that he is able to get himself out of bed is a tremendous milestone. Although he does not do this feat everyday, I am thrilled that he can do this by himself. When he doesn't get up on his own, I usually let him sleep until 9:30am. Then I carefully pull the blankets off to signal that it's time to get up. He does need to take medication in the morning and at night; therefore he should arise at a reasonable time.

Finally during the late spring of 2012, the C-Diff is finally conquered. But during the next year, Russ would have problems with constipation and diarrhea. His family doctor recommended laxatives but they only worked part of the time. I added probiotics to his daily regimen. Unfortunately, he dislikes yogurt so I resort to a powdered probiotic that is added to his Boost supplement drink.

The year 2013 has its ups and downs. Russ struggled to maintain a good weight in spite of eating well. He was so thin, it looked frightening. I mentioned it to the family doctor who recommended a gastroenterologist and later an endocrinologist. The gastroenterologist ordered a colonoscopy that revealed a small polyp. This was removed and tested positive for abnormal cells. He would have to get a repeat colonoscopy in another 5 years. Fatigue was another major problem for him. Sometimes he would just about fall asleep while eating supper. Each day was different. A good day consisted of him getting up on his own, playing cards and/or Connect Four, answering some questions correctly on *Are You Smarter Than A Fifth Grader?* A bad day found him sleeping much of the day. I finally accepted that this would be our life from now on. This was a much different picture of the retirement I had hoped for. I tried to keep a positive outlook, although I admit that some days this was a very difficult thing to do.

Final Thoughts

Experts talk about the stages of loss. Even though Russ did survive, I found myself going through these stages. The first stage, denial, occurred immediately after his cardiac arrest. I couldn't believe that my physically strong husband lay helpless in a hospital bed, barely alive. Later on, I denied the fact that his motor and cognitive skills were for the most part, changed forever. I kept hoping for the miracle that time and exercise would restore a majority of these skills. The next stage, anger, surfaced when I learned of the rumors and misinformation circulating in our community. It was further intensified by the indifference of our so-called friends. Before this time, I rarely got angry but now I still struggle with it. The grief stage was an especially prolonged one. It meant that our dreams of an ideal retirement would have to be modified. We could still travel but Russ's disability had to be taken into consideration. He needed his wheelchair for longer distances. I also grieved for the man I lost that April night. The man who could fix almost anything, take care of his own needs and was so independent now could not operate any machinery, be left unattended or remember neighbors. It took me almost 2 years to get through this grief. But at last I did reach the acceptance stage. Russ is still around to keep my company, to enjoy music and share in the good times we have going out to eat or visit relatives. He is in many ways the same man I married years ago. His motor and cognitive skills are restricted but he can still charm people with flattery. The acceptance meant that my constant crying was over, for the most part. There are the rare days when I still feel sorry for Russ and myself. It's on those days when the tears flow. I quickly remind myself to stop and remember the things we should be grateful for. Against all odds, he survived. I managed to pay all our bills and take care of household chores, including some repairs.

Many people have been amazed by my emotional strength during Russ's health crisis. I honestly don't know how I made it through the first few weeks when Russ was in a coma. God, Stephanie and Kip were a tremendous help in maintaining my sanity. I've always been emotionally strong but this crisis tested me in a way I could never imagine. There were moments, like when Russ had C-Diff , that I almost reached the limits of sanity. But something like a call from Stephanie would make the worst times bearable.

Although people marveled at my ability to cope, I did get impatient and angry at times, feeling guilty afterwards. At times, I asked the question, why me and why Russ? Russ also had his emotional challenges. One evening at dinner, he knocked over his glass of milk. I started to cry as I cleaned up the mess and so did Russ. We had been under so much stress. I rarely saw him cry before this time. I stopped and hugged him. It's as if we took comfort in each other. We both had a good cry after which I told him that we would get through this together. This is something we probably needed. I told him everything would be ok but I know that I couldn't guarantee it.

My family doctor gently suggested that a sedative or counseling might be helpful for me, considering what I've been through. I never cared for prescription medication so that was out of the question and as for counseling; Stephanie served as my "counselor". Whenever I felt that I couldn't cope, she gave me hope. I would not feel comfortable talking to someone outside the family. Let me make this clear, although I got through this crisis without medication or counseling, I realize that these are helpful for some individuals. Each of us has various abilities to cope. Sometimes prescription medication and/or a counselor to vent to are very helpful. But I know what works for me. If I feel the need for outside help in the future, then I will seek it.

Soon after Russ's cardiac arrest and brain injury, I realized that it would be up to me to learn more about his condition. The doctors answered some questions in general terms. But for specifics, I turned to the Internet to learn about anoxic brain injury. There was sufficient information on traumatic brain injury but less on anoxic brain injury. I soon learned about the levels of coma and the Rancho Los Amigos scale that is used to describe the stages of recovery after a brain injury. I then printed the information and put it in a folder. I soon had many folders where I kept information on brain injury, resources, social security disability and medical records. These folders soon overtook my desk so I bought a vertical file consisting of a dozen colored drawers. This made it easier to stay organized. Every file was in it's own drawer and was therefore accessible. My need to be organized was fulfilled. An Internet search yielded a wonderful article, *What Brain Injury Survivors Want You To Know.* I made a copy and attached it to my bathroom mirror. It served to remind me to be patient with Russ since brain injury survivors need additional time to do the tasks the rest of us take for granted.

I also learned to educate myself about the resources available for disabled people. While Russ was in the nursing home, I secured all the documents needed to secure veteran benefits. I turned to the agency for seniors in our town but was not given the correct information. Another agency for the disabled in town was more helpful. The social worker from the nursing service helped me sign up for the little known state assistance program. When Russ was released from the hospital and then the nursing home, I felt like we were thrown out into unfamiliar territory without any assistance. I believe that there should be more support from all social workers involved to help patients chart these unfamiliar "waters". Most of what I learned I stumbled upon through my own research. Brain injury happens quickly, leaving families in shock and having to make major decisions about their loved one's care. More support from the medical community is definitely needed.

Russ and I live in what I call "the new normal". This consists of frequent doctor appointments, using the walker for short walks and the wheelchair for longer excursions. It means that I must now do all the driving since I had the state revoke his driver's license. I doubt that he will ever be able to perform the complexities of driving a car. I do the house maintenance including mowing the yard and making minor repairs. If I do not have the expertise to do certain tasks, I hire others to do it. Russ's fatigue and his cognitive limitations hamper what he can do. I attempt to make his life as full as possible. We go to concerts, sit and walk outside plus we have even taken a few trips. When he is having a good day, we play Uno, Connect Four and Bingo. Although he is in some ways different from the man I married I still love him and enjoy his company. I am his caregiver, wife and above all his best friend.

I never dreamt that I would be a caregiver. Both my parents died years ago and so did any responsibility for their care. My role as caregiver is a reluctant, but necessary one. I still debate any decision I make about Russ's condition. *Should I push him to walk more? Is today's fatigue just part of the brain injury or something more?* Caregiving has been the most difficult undertaking that I've ever experienced. It's full of frustration, impatience and yet joy at times. Nevertheless I have no regrets about fighting for his survival. It has been an incredible journey for both of us. We have been through hell and emerged stronger in our love for one another. Russ, at times, tells me that he loves me. That feeling makes everything worthwhile.

For Stephanie

When my world was falling apart
your daily calls kept it together
You were an oasis in a sea
of turmoil.
I cried, you comforted me
When I needed someone to listen,
you were there.
When others turned away,
I could always count on you.
Although far away, I felt your presence
and support.
A card from you seemed to come
when I needed it the most.
Your gift of a simple necklace engraved
with the word hope reminds me never
to give up.
Thank you sweet daughter, for being
a perfect expression of love.

A Lost Friendship

I remember the good times,
the laughter we shared during
a Sunday morning breakfast
at a local diner,
The fun we had on a trip to a
East coast wedding.
You even helped us pack for a
nearby move.
But now the good times are over.
When we needed your friendship
and support, you seemed to disappear.
The past few years have been devoid
of any contact from you, even though
you are only a mile away.
It is painful to think we meant so little
to you.
The good times are gone and so is
your presence.

On Being Ignored

I saw you both,
sitting with your neighbors
at the pot luck dinner.
As we walked in
you did not look our way
even though I know you saw us.
In earlier years, you always
called to make sure we were
coming to the current pot luck
so we could sit together.
Even when you went to get
your dinner, your eyes turned
away from us.
There were others too who did
 not acknowledge our presence.
Others who were helped by a now
disabled man.
Your silent inaction hurt more than
Any cruel words ever could

Memories from before

I remember the great times together:
Our early morning walk in Anaheim
to buy Disneyland tickets.
Sitting on an Oahu beach watching
the sunset.
Admiring the majesty of the Rockies,
Getting sprayed and hearing the gushing
waters of Niagara Falls.
Watching the incoming boats in
South Haven.
I cherish these memories and smile,
knowing you are still here.
.

Evil C-Diff

C-Diff, you are the epitome of a
vicious, cunning scoundrel.
You strike your victims without
warning, making them weak and
miserable.
When it appears that you have been
defeated, you are in fact hiding in some
corner of the bowel, just waiting to
pounce upon the unwilling host.
You play this evil game repeatedly
until an army of good antibiotics and
probiotics overwhelm your thick, defensive
wall.
Do not be arrogant, C-Diff, for your days
are numbered.

Hope

This simple four-letter word that defied
the dismal prediction of the doctors.
It triumphed when the man responded to
requests to wiggle his toes and squeeze
their fingers.
When he took his first breath unassisted,
hope prevailed.
It was victorious when the man took his
first steps.
Hope did not give up and neither did
the man.

RESOURCES

biausa.org (Brain Injury Association Of America)- This website promotes advocacy, provides information on brain injury and has links to state brain injury affiliates. It also lists the location of each state's brain injury support groups.

BrainandSpinalCord.org- A good source of information about anoxic brain injury.

braininjuryguide.org- A very informative website containing facts about anoxic brain injury, available resources and consumer tips.

brain-injury-online.com- Facts about brain injury, stories from survivors and/or their families.

va.gov- This Veterans Administration website contains valuable information about services and benefits for veterans and their families.

VeteransAid.org- A website that has tips on applying for veterans benefits. It also has printable forms that are necessary to send to the Veterans Administration. There is also a forum in which members share tips and experiences securing benefits.

caregiver.com- This is a place for caregivers to share tips and stories. A newsletter and a magazine are also available.

n4a.org- Area Agencies On Aging are listed here, by state. These agencies can be contacted about initiating home and community based waiver programs for senior citizens. It also has useful information on housing and caregiving.

www.usa.gov/Topics/Seniors.shtml- A comprehensive list of information about health, housing, laws, caregiver resources and consumer protection for senior citizens.

home and community based waivers- Search this term to find state waiver programs that provide services to disabled seniors and/or children. These waivers help them remain in their home. Income guidelines apply.

www.ingramcontent.com/pod-product-compliance
Lightning Source LLC
Chambersburg PA
CBHW070640030426
42337CB00020B/4092